# Localized History Series

Clifford L. Lord, Editor

## Already Published:

| | |
|---|---|
| Teaching History with Community Resources (Second Edition) | *Clifford L. Lord* |

STUDENTS' GUIDES TO LOCALIZED HISTORY

| STATES: | | |
|---|---|---|
| | California | *Andrew Rolle* |
| | Colorado | *Carl Ubbelohde* |
| | Delaware | *John A. Munroe* |
| | Georgia | *James C. Bonner* |
| | Hawaii | *Gerrit P. Judd* |
| | Idaho | *Merle W. Wells* |
| | Kansas | *Nyle H. Miller* |
| | Kentucky | *Thomas D. Clark* |
| | Louisiana | *Joe Gray Taylor* |
| | Massachusetts | *William J. Reid* |
| | Minnesota | *Russell W. Fridley* |
| | New Hampshire | *James Duane Squires* |
| | New Jersey | *Richard P. McCormick* |
| | North Carolina | *William S. Powell* |
| | Ohio | *Francis P. Weisenburger* |
| | Oklahoma | *A. M. Gibson* |
| | Pennsylvania | *S. K. Stevens* |
| | Rhode Island | *Clifford P. Monahon* |
| | Tennessee | *William T. Alderson* |
| | Wisconsin | *Doris H. Platt* |
| | Wyoming | *Lola M. Homsher* |

| CITIES: | | |
|---|---|---|
| | Los Angeles | *Andrew Rolle* |
| | New York City | *Bayrd Still* |

| WATERSHEDS: | | |
|---|---|---|
| | The Upper Mississippi | *Walter Havighurst* |
| | The Ohio | *R. E. Banta* |
| | The Sacramento Valley | *Joseph A. McGowan* |

| PEOPLES: | | |
|---|---|---|
| | The Germans | *Carl Wittke* |
| | The Greeks | *Theodore Saloutos* |
| | The Norwegians | *Einar Haugen* |

## In Preparation:

| STATES: | | |
|---|---|---|
| | Alabama | *Charles G. Summersell* |
| | Alaska | *Bruce Le Roy* |
| | Arizona | *Bert M. Fireman* |
| | Connecticut | *Theodore Powell* |
| | Florida | *Samuel Proctor* |
| | Illinois | *Olive S. Foster* |
| | Maryland | *Harold Manakee* |

# LOCALIZED HISTORY SERIES

*Further Titles in Preparation:*

STATES:

| | |
|---|---|
| Mississippi | *John Hebron Moore* |
| Missouri | *Duane Meyer* |
| Montana | *Margery Brown* |
| Nebraska | *Donald F. Danker* |
| New Mexico | *James T. Forrest* |
| New York | *Marvin Rapp* |
| Oregon | *Thomas Vaughan* |
| South Dakota | *Herbert Schell* |
| Texas | *Frances J. Nesmith* |
| Utah | *Everett L. Cooley* |
| Vermont | *Graham S. Newell* |
| Washington | *Bruce Le Roy* |

CITIES:

| | |
|---|---|
| Boston | *Walter Muir Whitehill* |
| Chicago | *Clement M. Silvestro* |
| Denver | *John D. Mitchell* |
| Houston | *Joe B. Frantz* |
| Miami | *Frank Sessa* |
| Milwaukee | *Charles N. Glaab* |
| Raleigh-Durham-Chapel Hill | *William S. Powell* |
| San Francisco | *Moses & Ruth S. Rischin* |

WATERSHEDS:

| | |
|---|---|
| The Arkansas | *Edwin C. McReynolds* |
| The Canadian | *A. M. Gibson* |
| The Cimarron | *Homer E. Socolofsky* |
| The Delaware | *S. K. Stevens* |
| The James | *Marvin Schlegel* |
| The Kansas | *Nyle H. Miller* |
| The Kentucky | *Thomas D. Clark* |
| The Missouri | *Merrill Mattes* |
| The Platte | *James C. Olson* |
| The Potomac | *Walter S. Sanderlin* |
| The San Joaquin | *Andrew Rolle* |
| The Snake | *Merle W. Wells* |
| The Susquehanna | *S. K. Stevens* |
| The Tennessee | *William T. Alderson* |
| The Wisconsin | *August Derleth* |

PEOPLES:

| | |
|---|---|
| The Finns | *John Kolehmainen* |
| The Irish | *Carl Wittke* |
| The Italians | *Rudolph J. Vecoli* |
| The Mexicans | *Carey McWilliams* |
| The Puerto Ricans | *Joseph Monserrat* |
| The Swedes | *Franklin D. Scott* |

CLIFFORD L. LORD

President,
Hofstra University

# TEACHING HISTORY
# WITH
# COMMUNITY RESOURCES

## Second Edition

*Teachers College Press*

Teachers College  Columbia University
New York, New York

# *Preface*

The vital need in this shrunken and fast-moving world is to get to know and understand both other peoples and ourselves. This is not the time in world history to send ignorant Americans abroad, nor to tolerate their domestic counterparts at home. It is the time to be better informed about—to understand—both others and ourselves.

To understand is not necessarily to accept, to adopt, or even to sympathize with. To understand *other* peoples is not necessarily to accept or adopt what they believe or stand for, any more than to understand the principles of Zen Buddhism or to comprehend what motivates the aggressions of an overly ambitious man is to accept either course of action for yourself. It is simply that if you understand other peoples (just like other individuals), it is easier to communicate, negotiate, do business with them, to enjoy their company, without the needless *faux pas* and irritations which ignorance can cause. If you know enough to put yourself in the other person's shoes, see things as he will see things, think as he will think, it is easier to arm yourself in advance with the answers to probable problems and to be ready to move more rapidly to the heart of whatever social, political, economic, or cultural matter is at hand—person to person, at home or abroad, or nation to nation. Here at home, if we are going to have an important conference with other Americans we have never met, we get all the information we can about them before we meet. We should do the same with other peoples. And school is the place to start the learning that leads to such understanding.

To understand *others,* we need to know as much as possible about their history, economy, society, culture, institutions, customs, literature, and languages. Their history is their present background, and to know their history is to understand how they became what they are. Their economy may be in a different state of development or under different types of controls from ours, and to understand

v

their economy is to understand the reasons for various policies and for certain national or public attitudes. The structure of their society explains why some things are possible today and others are not. And so with their culture, customs, institutions, literature. Each offers many keys to understanding. Thus for perhaps a generation we have had courses and materials at all levels about other peoples. Elementary readers tell us about Eskimos and Italians and New Zealanders and Arabs. We have courses in peoples of the world and surveys of world history. In college we have world history, comparative government, area studies, and French or Chinese or other national literature. Increasingly we study foreign languages at all levels as a key both to communication and to understanding. And we have a burgeoning program of area institutes and special programs at the graduate level.

To help us understand *ourselves,* we have elementary school units on family and community; secondary school courses which include problems of democracy, American history, economics, geography, and American literature; and more elaborate offerings at college and graduate levels. But aside from the rudimentary courses in community and family, so often given in the fourth or fifth grade, we largely ignore one of the most effective and important areas for gaining an understanding of ourselves: the local scene.

This really is paradoxical. We war on poverty; we bulldoze our slums; we applaud massive programs of aid to education and social welfare programs of a scope undreamed of before the latter half of the twentieth century; we explore outer space and inner space, and rapidly approach the day when the doctor's chief problem will be not how to keep a person alive but when to let him die. We are creating problems of an enormity unique to this generation (atomic annihilation, air and water pollution, the population explosion for a few examples); we have created in the United States the most affluent society in history, an increasingly effective approach to a truly democratic society whose proudest boast will be genuine equality of opportunity; we spend billions of dollars without blinking an eye; we not long ago were the envy of the world, and still are for a very large sector. Yet we do very, very little to understand ourselves, to understand how all this could come to be in these United States. This is where the local scene is *so* important.

No one seriously disputes the pedagogical value of using local materials in the social studies. Something near at hand—a tool, a newspaper, a letter, a building, the local police department, the freight yard, the common council, the nearby museum—to illustrate a point, to introduce a new topic, or to open new horizons—is always useful. Because it is close by rather than remote, because it is seen rather than unseen, the student can often feel and always sense more than just what a book or the teacher can tell him. His curiosity is more easily aroused, he is more apt to be stimulated to serious and original thinking. A cow looks and certainly smells differently in the flesh from in the dictionary. So does a locomotive. A common council or a legislature in action is a much more human institution than the textbook descriptions may suggest. We understand this so well that we introduce the social studies at the primary level through studies of the intimate: the family and community. But in later school years we often let this invaluable source of stimulation and insight go by default. This is silly. Across the country, a few of the best teachers of the social studies appreciate the value of local materials and continue to utilize them throughout the primary, intermediate, and secondary grades. It is the purpose of this book to suggest some of the ways this has been and can be done.

Obviously, school curricula vary considerably from community to community and from state to state. They even vary considerably in a single school system at the hands of different teachers. The following pages are addressed to the teaching profession generally. The discerning teacher will pick and choose, select and modify, according to the age and ability levels of his or her students. And though addressed to the teacher, the material is equally useful to the superior high school student who, for advanced credit, as a junior historian, or simply to satisfy his own curiosity, wants to use community resources for his own edification, enlightenment, and understanding.

No one class, no one school can do all the things suggested. The smorgasbord of community resources is tantalizingly rich and varied. Yours is the privilege of choosing what best fits the needs of your particular school, or class, or group. If you are interested in more "content" in the social studies offerings, here is content galore.

# Contents

# 1

## By Way of
## Background

HISTORY is a huge and fascinating subject. *Huge* because, though once largely a matter of politics and wars, it now covers the gamut of man's activities, his hopes and aspirations, his successes and failures, since records (inscriptions, tablets, and certain types of archeological remains) came into being. Every nation, every race, every continent has its history; every "age" has a history. So does every building, farm, road, school, church, store, partnership, company, corporation. Project this back over four millenia to the beginnings of written records, and you have a lot of territory to cover. *Fascinating* because it is the record of mankind and only one thing fascinates man more than does nature (the world around him) : that is man himself.

## The Field of History

Years ago the historian had only the rather sizable task of exhuming from the records—relatively scarce for ancient history, incredibly prolific for the present day—the evidence from which to piece together the particular segment of history on which he was at work. Now he needs to know political science, because government obviously is important to the story of mankind. He needs to know economics, because ever since man began to produce a surplus of any kind and market it, since he developed barter and currency and commerce, economics has become increasingly important to his history. He needs to know geography, for without a comprehension of the location of natural resources, natural routes of transportation and communication, topography, soil, and climate, he will lack essential background for the story of human events in a given area. He needs to know anthropology, the science of the types and races of mankind, man's geographic and historic distribution, his relationship to his environment and his culture, if he is to understand any phase of history in relation to the broad outlines of human development. He needs to know sociology, the science of the origins and evolution of society, and of the forms, institutions, functions, and collective behavior of human groups, if he is to understand a

2

phase of history in terms of collective behavior or social developments. He needs to know psychology, the science of the mind of man and of the phenomena of individual human behavior, if he is to understand or speculate about the motivation of the person or the group he is studying. History, then, has once again become the queen of the social sciences, the one which draws upon and utilizes all the others.

Because history is so vast and complicated a discipline, only a Toynbee, a Spengler, or a McGill can range the whole field. Most historians specialize in a part or field of history. The traditional divisions are by era: ancient history— no longer just Greece and Rome, but one of the most rapidly developing fields of all as we decipher previously incomprehensible writings like those of the Hittites or the Incas, as carbon 14 brings accurate chronology to artifacts and eras at whose age we earlier could only guess; medieval history; modern European; American. To these must now be added Chinese history, that of the subcontinent of India, North Africa, sub-Sahara Africa, Russia, Latin America, Japan, perhaps Polynesia, as a minimum. The traditional fields, and most of their newer counterparts, are further divided into periods: the Age of Pericles, or the Ming Dynasty; the Renaissance, the Reformation; the Stuarts and Tudors, or the Empire; the French, Industrial, Agricultural, Transportation, Russian Revolutions; the Colonial, Federal, Middle Periods, etc.

Within the chronological divisions are divisions by approach. There is narrative history: the story of a dynasty, a nation, a bank, railroading, a war, a particular day (when Lincoln died, D-Day, when the *Lusitania* sank, etc.). There is biography: the story of a man or a woman, prominent or otherwise, good or not so good. (Some people say they write biographies of companies or colleges or churches. But others could with equal inexactness say they write biographies of nations or civilizations, and then—as so often happens when analogies are pressed too far—there would be no distinction left. Biography is the story of an individual being and his activities, his impact on events and thought.)

There is still another basis for dividing history—a geographical basis. This produces world history, or western (or other) civilization, or national history, or what we now call localized history. This last is the history of the community, county, or region. Or it is the history of government, or industry (or an industry), or communication, or public welfare, or medicine, or education, or an organization, or a church, or a farm, or a mine, or individuals within this state-or-smaller range. And here is where, in any school district or its immediate environs, a wealth of stimulating and provocative material is readily available for the imaginative teacher and the perceptive student.

## The Historian and His Work

Historians range in age from the very young to the very old. They may be highly trained in the techniques of the profession, or they may be beginners— like some of the amateurs in the local historical society, like the pupils in the local junior high school or in the fourth grade.

What does the historian do? A major part of his job is to reconstruct the past; but how does he find out what happened? He works from records. Records may be the clay tablets of the archives at Nineveh or Bogozköy, or hieroglyphs on the walls of the Temple of Karnak, or inscriptions on Roman arches, or monkish script on parchment or vellum. They may be the ruins of an old saw-mill, an adze or a flintlock, a town ordinance, an account book, a newspaper, a diary, a letter; the taped reminiscences of a participant in the Manhattan Project or the New Deal, or of an early settler, or of the reformer whose agitation upset the local political machine seventeen years ago. They may be a Spanish mission in California or a wooden Russian Orthodox church in Alaska; a feather cape in the Bishop Museum in Honolulu or a New England coverlet; an A-drag from a pioneer farm or a branding iron from a huge cattle ranch; a letter from a great-great-great uncle in the California gold rush or a grandfather in World War I; the diary of an itinerant evangelist or the ostensorium left at Green Bay by the explorer Perrot; a railroad timetable of 1870 or the letters home from the immigrant in America; a painting in a cave in Spain, or a folk-painting of an Eastman or a Bingham; a Currier and Ives print or a photograph; a speech, a sermon, a novel based on conditions in the stockyards or the back streets of the metropolis or the quiet New England village. All offer evidence of man's activities of one kind or another.

But, as any lawyer knows, there are many kinds of evidence. And some evidence often conflicts with other evidence. Try staging an incident in the classroom. Tell the students to watch closely, and half an hour later have them write an account of precisely what happened. They will be surprised at how greatly the accounts differ, and they will gain a valuable lesson about evidence which will stand them in good stead whenever they have to make judgments in school and college, or in later life.

The historian has to go by the best available evidence; he has to judge. Some historical evidence is incontrovertible. The date of Lincoln's signing of the Emancipation Proclamation is not open to question; the original document exists and is clearly dated. The time and place of the surrender of the Japanese at the end of World War II is not open to question. The document is dated; there were a great many people there, and the newspapers and newsreels were full of the story. But what the Governor of North Carolina said to the Governor of South Carolina is debatable. Man's memory is notoriously unreliable, and where we are dependent on recollection or on memoirs written long after the event we are on perilous ground. A newspaper account is not always reliable, as we all know. And the opinions of batter and umpire frequently differ as to whether that pitch was or was not in the strike zone.

So the historian constantly has to make judgments about his evidence. Did this man have an ulterior motive in recording this event this way? Does the internal evidence support the authenticity of the document or the truth of the story? Is the Kensington Runestone authentic or a fake? How about the Cardiff Giant? Or the Protocols of Zion? Or Mr. Washington's cherry tree? Was Andrew Johnson as bibulous as the Radical Republicans sought to make the country believe? Was Herbert Hoover as incompetent as the Democrats in the 1932 campaign said? Was there a missile gap in 1960? The superficial evidence may be conflicting. The historian has to judge.

Many years ago, some historians thought of their subject as a science. Their idea was that you could gather and test historical data the way you would test scientific data in the laboratory. They thought that if you could get enough evidence you could reconstruct the past fully, completely, accurately. We are not so sure of that today. Men's motives are often elusive. The evidence is seldom complete, seldom without contradictions, is sometimes rigged or even forged. Words do not always mean what they seem to say—witness propaganda, Hitler's technique of the "big lie," the use of false or misleading advertising, Communist "double-think"—and they often do not mean to another generation what they meant to their own. Even statistics—hard, cold figures—can be and have been used to support substantially contradictory conclusions.

So we think today of history as both science and art: science in that the historian like a scientist develops imaginative, speculative, intuitive hypotheses and then, using a scientific approach to evidence, tests those hypotheses against the evidence; art in that the historian aspires to a craftsmanship through which his acquired skills of understanding and insight into how individuals or groups or societies are apt to act under certain circumstances can be used to interpret the carefully weighed evidence and then to paint the scene, the event, the conference, the battle, the era with the broad strokes which make it come alive and stir the minds of others. Well done, history can be every bit as stimulating as art or music or literature: this is the story of mankind, which nothing can excel for the excitement or provocation of thought and meditation. From Galileo and Copernicus to the conquest of space, from Galen and Hippocrates to modern medicine, from debtors' prison to bankruptcy laws, from education for the privileged to free public schools, from serfdom and slavery to equality of opportunity, from sand paintings to Michelangelo, from sod-house to skyscraper, from canoe to hydrofoil, from horseback to jet aircraft, from the invention of the wheel to the harnessing of the power of the fission of the atom, history, despite man's occasional and provocative lapses into barbarism, is a stimulating panorama. How in the midst of Oriental despotisms tiny Greek states could emerge with concepts of individual freedom; how man could develop the systems of capital and banking and insurance; how the idea of the state could evolve from despotism to democracy, from autocracy to serving the general welfare; how relationships between states could move from anarchy to at least concepts of law and order, treaties, world courts, and rudimentary international legislation: these, again despite the setbacks, excite the imagination. And their portrayal calls for more than the skilled technician; it calls for the great artist.

## Values of History

Great artists among historians are as rare as great artists in the fine arts, but a knowledge and appreciation of history is important to just about everyone. Why?

Because a knowledge of how and why the Negro first came in large numbers to this country, his conditions of living in terms not just of forced labor but of the impact of slavery on mind and spirit and family and ethics, the mishandling of the freedmen in the bitter power contest between Radicals and Bourbons after the Civil War, the conditions of inequality bred by the doctrine of "equal but separate" facilities, is essential to an understanding of later demands for civil rights, integrated facilities, equal job opportunities.

Because a knowledge of Russian history at least back to the liberation of the serfs, through the development of the Russian economy under the Czars, the October Revolution, the philosophies of Marx, Lenin, and Trotsky, the driving despotism of Stalin, the organization and posture of Communism both in Russia and elsewhere, is essential in order to understand the prejudices of the Soviet Union, the nature of the Communist threat and the Cold War, the real problems of world peace.

Because knowledge of how the development of the American economy is related to the impetus supplied by the Civil and subsequent wars; to the presence of rich natural resources; to the huge supply of cheap labor available in the days of unrestricted immigration; to the unmistakable connection between the chance of large cash rewards and the appearance of a plethora of inventive, entrepreneurial, and managerial genius; to the growth of huge business, abortively through trusts, later through diversification; to the responding growth of organized labor; to the resulting high productivity and remarkable standard of living; and to the implications of automation, is essential to prepare for the critical problems of the truly affluent society of unlimited production which we soon may face.

The point is that history is important because it gives us the background of—helps us understand—present problems.

History also gives us perspective. In the shorter run, it may curb aggressive impatience if we realize where real wages were in the United States in 1900 as compared with 1950, and in 1950 as compared with the present day; if we recognize the degree to which the classless society has emerged in this country since the turn of the century, over and above the formal democracy and the very real opportunities of the nineteenth century; if we contrast the status of immigrant and minority groups fifty years ago with their status today; if we compare the general level of American culture then and now. In the somewhat longer run, it gives perspective to look at the United States of, say, 1850 and to note the change from a predominantly agrarian, small-town civilization to the present predominantly urban culture, where no community is isolated from the radio or telephone, where few are out of reach of television, and where the steel bands that in 1850 were beginning to bind the nation together and to give new mobility to raw materials, finished products, and people are already largely supplanted by ribbons of concrete and jet trails in the air. And in the long run, it gives perspective to watch the growth of the medieval city and its market place, and its economic, social, and ultimately political effects; to note the impact of Renaissance and Reformation on economics and society as well as on culture and the emancipation of the mind; to see the evolution of western civilization through the Ages of Reason and Enlightenment, through industrial and agricultural and technological revolutions, through general literacy and broader and deeper education, through increasing democracy and more equal opportunity, through its world-wide impact in the twentieth century, to the extraordinary days which loom just ahead. History shows us where we've been—how we got where we are.

It also teaches us humility. The ruins of ancient Egypt, of the Hittites, of Knossos and Chaldea, of Aztecs and Khmers, indeed of Greece and Rome, remind us how transitory a particular civilization can be. The achievement of a Mosaic Code, the Christian ethic, Aristotelian logic, Ptolemaic astronomy, Chinese printing, or Aztec calendars suggests forcefully that not all wisdom and all brilliance have been bestowed on the present generation or on western civilization. It makes one question the arrogance of those who condemn President Buchanan for playing for time and not forcing a showdown on the issues which led to the Civil War: what, indeed, would they have done in his shoes? Or the superficiality of those who condemn all aspects of colonialism as totally bad. Or the patent absurdity of any theory of the inevitability of history.

Finally, history gives us a sense of roots, of belonging. Of belonging to the stream of history, of the evolution of man from primordial ooze or later primeval forest to his present state. Of belonging to a great civilization—in many ways, as it should be, the greatest yet. Of belonging to a great nation, in a sense today as in Lincoln's day the last best hope of mankind. Of belonging to a citizenry involved in the solution of vast and complex problems surely no more vexing than those facing Lincoln on the eve of civil war or his successors at its end. In a time of great mobility of persons, of mass migrations and population displacements, in an era when the threat of mass self-destruction over-hangs mankind, when concepts of relativity make uncertain the seemingly ob-vious, and when changing customs challenge accepted moral values, this sense of belonging to something big and great is of enormous importance. Along with it is apt to come the sense of being able, indeed obliged, to contribute one's bit to the evolution of that civilization or that nation—or, as we shall see, to one's community.

Thus, if history brings us to understand others and so to work with them or at least to understand their premises and prejudices; if it brings us to under-stand ourselves and our government, economy, society, and culture; if it gives us the background of present problems, perspective and humility, and a sense of inheriting and participating in a great national undertaking and a great civilization; surely it has the capacity to inculcate real wisdom. This is no small order. This is the importance of the study of history.

## Values of Localized History

Localized history represents the smallest geographical unit of the study of history. It is the history of the community, the town, the city, the local area, the county, the neighboring region. Its field is smaller than the state (state history), larger than the individual (biography). Its topics are those of gen-eral history: political, social, economic, cultural, military, educational, religious, scientific, medical, intellectual.

Localized history has all the values of general history. It, too, brings us to understand ourselves—more intimately, certainly, than general history. It, too, gives us perspective and humility and a sense of inheriting and participating in an ongoing project of some antiquity—something of peculiar importance to the mobile and rootless young. It, too, inculcates at least a localized wisdom.

But localized history goes further than that. It makes contributions, has values, peculiarly its own.

### ILLUSTRATION OF NATIONAL TRENDS

One special merit is that it supplies illustrative material for every phase of national history that touches your locality. You don't expect to study the details of the lumbering industry in the Mojave desert, nor the impact of slavery on Alaska. But wherever there are people there is history. Who they are, how they got there, why they are there, how they have earned a living, how they have governed themselves, what they have done with their spare time and with their minds; these and a hundred other aspects of their localized history will give new insights into the story of the United States. Here is where you illustrate the national generalization with the local specific.

## SUSPICION OF GENERALIZATIONS

But here is also where you check the generalization against the local specific and find some remarkable variations on the theme. A few instances:

We talk glibly of the influence of the railroads in tying the nation together with bands of steel, in bringing a new and cheap mobility to goods and thus creating a national market, in making it possible for people to travel, on business as well as pleasure, at new speeds for newly great distances. But if we focus on a community, we see what the railroad really means in its effect on business, on industry, on banking, on employment. Or, in the community it bypassed, we see the withering that resulted from being cut off from these new main arteries of commerce. And we come to understand better why towns bid against each other for the railroad's favor, why farms were mortgaged to determine its route, why rate differentials were a matter of such vital concern.

We generalize about the changed role of women in industry and agriculture occasioned by the departure of so much of the male population for the Civil War. In the community we see it happen. We can note the changes in local industry, too, the acceleration of mechanization, the impact of war contracts. We can note specific examples of the effect of the huge war traffic on the young railroads.

We deprecate or admire the ruthlessness with which growing monopolies and trusts forced competitors to the wall. In the community, we can see what this meant to the people in both the short and the long run: in employment, in prices, in taxes, perhaps later in relief rolls.

We talk of automation and its effects and ramifications. In the community, we can study the supermarket or the automated factory or the telephone service in terms of its impact on the community and its people.

We look at our political parties at the local level. We find local leaders of a party urging economy where the same party nationally is advocating heavy spending; local leaders seeking a higher tariff on a local product while the national party is sponsoring tariff reduction; local leaders seeking disaster relief, or rural renewal, or federal aid to education, while the national party is calling for reduced federal spending; local leaders opposing desegregation while their national leaders—and their local counterparts in other areas—are urging it. Putting our parties under the microscope reveals that they are not great monolithic organizations but federations of state organizations which in turn are federations of local organizations. If communities differ one from another—as they do—because their people have made them different, their interests will be different, and local political leadership must reflect those differences. State organizations and national parties therefore are at best confederations of local groups and local leaders who may agree on many things but are going to differ

radically on others. State legislatures and the U.S. Congress are not in fact remote, Olympian bodies, but consist of representatives of the localities (House)
and— in Congress—the states (Senate) and their respective interests. This is
what makes the legislative process in a democracy so fascinating and so intricate, and so worth studying and understanding.

We speak of the Westward movement and give the impression that migration (aside from the farm to city movement) was all westward. Localized history in the appropriate communities will show United Empire Loyalists fleeing
the Revolution northward to Canada, or like Benedict Arnold eastward to England; leaders of the Confederacy seeking refuge southward in Latin America
or eastward in Europe; Mennonite groups moving northward from Pennsyl-
vania into Ontario; westward migrants returning to the old country; individuals
moving into a given community from north, south, east, and west. Church records of membership transfer can be fascinating in this regard.

The South seceded from the Union in 1861, but communities, not just in
what became West Virginia but all through the Tennessee Valley (including
northern Alabama), the Cumberland Mountains, the German-settled areas of
Texas, voted strongly against secession, while other areas like the Irish-dominated
Free State of Jones (Mississippi) seceded from the Confederacy and maintained
their independence for some time during the Civil War.[1]

Tobacco is chiefly grown south of the Mason-Dixon Line and the Ohio
River. But the student of a community in the Connecticut Valley, southern
Ohio and Illinois, the Finger Lakes region of New York, southern Wisconsin,
or northwestern Missouri knows that it is also grown there.

Wherever you turn in localized history, not only do you find local, tangible,
understandable illustrations of the national generalization, but you find other
developments which are quite the opposite. From this comes, obviously, a
healthy skepticism about the glib generalization and a new appreciation of the
diversity of the American scene. These are two of the special values of the study
of localized history.

## UNDERSTANDING THE AMERICAN EXPERIMENT

A third derives from the fact that localized history puts man and his activities under the microscope. The microscopic approach is quite as revealing in the
social sciences as in the natural. Every community has a history of its own—different, special, and significant. The history of some communities may be more
important, i.e., have more impact than others (for example, Buffalo, N.Y., vs.
Buffalo, Wyo.), but each has its own significance in helping understand the
American experiment, its society, economy, and polity. In this specific instance,

[1] See map #148 in Lord and Lord, *Historical Atlas of the U. S.* (New York, 1953),
p. 93.

the second largest city in New York State, western terminus of the Erie Canal and a great railroad center, with a university and two colleges, once with a large population of immigrants and now with many second-generation Americans, with suburbs and the problems of suburban growth and services, with light and heavy industry and major shipping facilities, has a rich and varied history. So, too, has Buffalo, Wyo., a little New England village with elm-lined common and white clapboard houses, located on Clear Creek below the red sandstone foothills of the Big Horns.

Every community has a complex history. It may seem simple, but only if it has never been investigated. It may be dominated in the public consciousness by a single event, but only because of the peculiar drama of that event. There is more to Plymouth than the landing of the Pilgrims; there is more to Trenton than a Revolutionary War battle; there is more to Freeport than a Lincoln-Douglas debate.

Every community is a monument to the men and women who made it: to the first settlers, who may or may not have fought Indians (those in Levittown, for instance, never had the pleasure); to the men who surveyed the streets and later paved them, then used them for the installation of water, sewer, and electric facilities; to the men who opened the first stores and those whose bright ideas and clever merchandising made big stores out of little ones; to the men who had an idea that became a shop and later a big industry, the town's major taxpayer and largest employer; to the editor who pilloried all transgression, real or imaginary, so mercilessly that for a generation he created a different climate of public morality and left behind a tradition with which others could conjure; to the minister whose evangelical zeal for the Social Gospel and for the dignity of every human being made the town a better place in which to live; to the patron whose generosity made possible special cultural opportunities in the town; to the teacher who opened new horizons to generation after generation of students. To the men and women who moved there from other lands, bringing with them not only wiener schnitzel and saurbraten, spaghetti and pizza, svenska chitbula and polish sausage, borscht and shish-kabob, but wonderful customs like the Czech family compact, the Polish New Year's family communion, sundry spring festivals, and other folk customs which slowly but surely have made or are making their way into our own American culture—just as those who brought them made their way into the American economy and society and polity, despite much heartache and discrimination, with major and visible success.

The microscopic approach lets us see how things happen: how, for instance, people's savings in local banks (or insurance premiums), or the accumulated capital of individuals or of businesses, may be reinvested in the community to offer new jobs, new payrolls, new first steps toward further savings which can be (directly or via the bank or insurance company) reinvested for further growth. It shows us very specific instances of people coming to the community from abroad, perhaps starting with manual or menial labor, joining ethnic benevolent societies and fraternal organizations, then rising in society and in earning power as they gain experience and usefulness (or as they are pushed upwards by the advent of less-skilled and less-experienced manual or menial labor), rearing sons and daughters who do much better for the most part and take an earned place higher up the economic, political, and social ladder.

Such an approach shows specifically how effective positive local leadership can be. It illustrates concretely what it takes to put across a reform (or any change in the law that somebody wants made). It brings into clear focus the individuals who make localized history: the political leader, the civic reformer, the advocate of parks and recreational facilities, the proposer of tax privilege which brings new industry to the community; the frontier marshal who establishes law and order; the district attorney who rids the community of the numbers racket; the minister or social worker who ends a juvenile crime wave; the banker who makes the decision which brings a new business to the community (or which perhaps forces an old one to close); the widow whose efforts bring a successful concert series to town; the fire chief whose insistence on efficiency in his department produces a most attractive local insurance rate; the leader in the local service club who gets his colleagues to set up a scholarship to send a local high school boy or girl annually to Europe for a year's study; the men who persuade the common council to change the zoning ordinance to permit an industrial park or high-rise apartments; the labor leader who sells new goals and new responsibilities to his union; the man or the group which forces a change in the local tax structure; the real estate promoter who opens a new subdivision; the community leaders who insist on a new high school or a civic auditorium and convention center or who establish an educational television station; the gallant souls who start legitimate theaters, or art galleries, or museums, or orchestras, or bookstores—usually before the community is really ready for them—and may have to struggle all their lives to keep them going until the population and leisure time and cultural appreciation grow to the point where such ventures are no longer in imminent danger of being forced to close their doors.

We all recognize that it does make a difference whether a Coolidge or a Franklin D. Roosevelt is president of the United States; whether a Chamberlain or a Churchill is Prime Minister of Great Britain; whether a Stalin or a Khrushchev is First Minister of the Soviet Union. Does it make no difference who is superintendent of schools (or principal of the individual school)? Does it make no difference whether the chief of police is a courageous and honest man or a crook? Does it make no difference what kind of man heads the bank, or the local industry, or the welfare department?

Localized history, in other words, is the story of the people who make local history: ordinary people like you and me, and some extraordinary people, too. People with the courage to pull up stakes and move west; people with the courage to cross the ocean to try for a better life in a strange country with a strange language, a strange law, strange customs; people with the courage to admit defeat and return east; people who gave up too easily and too soon. People with the imagination to invent something the world could use right then, at that very time; people with the imagination to see an opportunity in business or service and grasp it; people so concerned with the general welfare that they sacrifice their own peace and quiet and that of their families to crusade for reform, for the elimination of abuse, for the more perfect world we all seek. People whose bright ideas are wrongly timed, whose invention is something for which the public has as yet no need, whose reform is ahead of its time, whose move in a particular field is ill-timed and so is condemned to failure. And people who cheat both others and themselves, who fail in what they attempt, who in failing slash about them and topple others with them. People who, after real success, after a genuine contribution, fall on evil days and live out the tragedy which the Greeks so clearly saw was the essence of man's battle with his environment, with circumstance, and with himself.

Obviously our institutions, being man-made, are the creations of people. And the corollary of the fact that people are different, one from another, is that our institutions are different, one from another. Our schools are different— their principals and teachers and boards have made them so. Our colleges are different—they are but the lengthening shadows of their leaders. Our corporations are different—the different degrees of imagination and daring (and sometimes luck) of their officers have made them so.

Our towns are different; their people have made them so. It is not just a matter of economic resources, though this makes a great difference in the potential of a community; it is a matter of people. Neighboring towns which begin with similar natural resources are different—in appearance, in occupations, in feel. Indeed, towns which are less favored in natural resources are sometimes more prosperous than their more favored neighbors. There are, for instance, two towns within thirty-five miles of each other on the Mississippi River. The first is long and narrow, built along a strip of land one block wide between the river and the bluffs. The other is on a broad alluvial plain at the confluence of the Mississippi and one of its substantial tributaries (thus having two big rivers, while the first town has one). The first town is on one main railroad, but the trains do not stop. The second is on two main lines, and the trains do stop. The population of the first is 900, of the second 5000. The first has neither bridge nor ferry across the Mississippi; the second has free bridges across both the Mississippi and its tributary. Neither has any geological resource except inexhaustible limestone. One would expect the larger town with all its natural and man-made advantages to be the more prosperous of the two. It is not. The imaginative leadership of one man who was mayor of the smaller town for over a quarter of a century made the difference. He brought a big power plant to his town by highly imaginative political and economic maneuvering. He brought a major historical park to his community which annually attracts thousands of visitors. He brought in smaller industry, developed resort facilities, brought prosperity to his river town. The larger community lacked such leadership, lost its only large industry, saw its taverns become its major economic resource. It is really no over-simplification to say that one individual was responsible for the difference in the history of these two adjacent towns for the past quarter-century.

The microscopic localized investigation of specific aspects of our society, economy, and democracy has tremendous potential. It gets us very close to the wellsprings of the American genius. It puts right before our eyes the basis of what made our economy so dynamic, so productive, resulting in a standard of living in a largely classless society which is the envy of the world. It shows us right in our own community what makes our society so fluid, so free of that rigidity of social structure which is still characteristic of western Europe and far more so of much of the rest of the world. It makes us see and understand the process of democracy in action and realize the importance of our boast of equality of opportunity for all Americans—and the importance of seeing that that boast has reality throughout the country. It shows us the secrets of the success of the American experiment. And this brings us close to a genuine understanding of our society, our economy, and our political forms—our way of life. This too is important.

## THE IMPORTANCE OF THE INDIVIDUAL

But this focus on people is of extraordinary significance in another way. In the hypotheses, synthesis, and generalizations so necessary to the writing of national (or western or world) history, people are all too often lost sight of. The individual becomes a mere statistic, often a mere cipher. Ciphers have a rather negative connotation. They smack of nothingness, of impotence, of not counting. And when people are treated as statistics or ciphers, the next step is to consider them unfit to govern themselves—a dictatorship of the elite (or in some quarters, of the proletariat) can do the job better. Localized history has its statistics and its ciphers too, but its focus is on the fact that ordinary people (not just presidents, cabinet officers, ambassadors, or generals) make history, influence the course of events where you can clearly see it—in the community or the county or the region.

You cannot study a community—or a corporation or a college or a church—and forget for a moment that people make its history. This gives concrete, tangible, specific meaning to the continuing importance of the individual. The same sort of thing happens on the national and international scene,[2] but that is

---

[2] See for instance, Oscar Handlin, *Chance or Destiny: Turning Points in American History* (Boston, 1955).

remote; the community is close at hand. It is often difficult to pinpoint responsibility in the complex bureaucracies of the national or world scene; it is relatively easy to see who is making things happen in one's own locality.

The importance of the individual is a tenet basic to western civilization and to the Judeo-Christian tradition. It is the opposite of the Communist (or Fascist) philosophy of the all-powerful state, which may exist for the theoretical benefit of the people, but in which the people have no voice as to what happens.

In an era when we are contesting for the minds and souls of mankind, when we are defending our concept of government as the servant of the people, and of the people as the repository of ultimate wisdom, it is of the utmost importance that we recognize and utilize these special values of localized history: (1) the close, visible, at-hand demonstration, from the days of first settlement on, of how our type of society, economy, and democracy operates; (2) the local visible specific to the national generalization; and (3) the equally visible and demonstrable evidence of the impact and importance of the individual. Here is, above all others, the area of study that shows what makes America "click." Here is the area of study that above all others hurls back in their teeth the arguments of those who would persuade us of the inevitability of history and those who believe that economic motivation is the exclusive determinant of man's actions. Those who study localized history know better. They know that change, the essense of the historical story, can of course be brought about by natural phenomena: a change of climate (the advent of an Ice Age or a Dust Bowl), or a local catastrophe (the eruption of Mt. Vesuvius or the flood which destroyed Jamestown, West Virginia). They know that the exhaustion of a gold deposit, or the supplanting of coal by oil for fuel, can force a major change in the history of the localities and people involved. But they also know that most change, for the better or for the worse, can be and is much more frequently brought about by the effort of individual men and women. They know, too, that these men and women are motivated by ideals, loyalties, fear, love, hate, and desire for recognition, as well as by the chance for profit and economic advantage.

This we must know and understand today and tomorrow. This factual understanding of what is central to the American experiment is essential if we are to be comprehensible, let alone convincing, to others; if we are to be able to defend intelligently the core of the American experiment against direct challenge, infiltration, subversion, or simple indifference—perhaps even more essential in periods of rapprochement and good feeling *vis à vis* the Soviet Union than in periods of Cold War. The student coming into first-hand contact with the importance of the individual on the local scene, with the multiplicity of human motivations, with the fact that change is created by individuals as well as by natural forces, is apt to be properly skeptical, when he meets them, of two basic tenets of Marxism: the totality and all-pervasiveness of economic motivation and the impotence of the individual who might therefore just as well surrender all individual independence and freedom to the paternalistic, all-powerful, all-wise state.

There is, therefore, no phase of social studies about America that cannot benefit from the use of localized materials for illustration, for investigation, for the achievement of greater understanding and wisdom. There also is no degree of student sophistication too high to benefit from this use of resources close at hand.

## Why is Localized History Not More Utilized?

If localized history does supply this intimate, immediate, microscopic understanding of the working and the dynamics of our economy, society, and democracy; if it indeed offers countless community examples of national developments and a healthy antidote to ready acceptance of generalizations; if it indeed indicates a great diversity of interests and developments within the American scene in any particular field and so teaches us that political parties, industries, regions, movements of all kinds are not great monolithic phenomena but contain within themselves the seeds of variety, dissent, and change; if it proves the continuing importance of the individual in an era of strong concentration of governmental and economic power; if it helps the youngest pupil and can challenge the most sophisticated, and if the materials are readily at hand, why is it not universally acclaimed as an essential part of every school curriculum?

There are several reasons.

"Local" history has acquired, with much justification, a bad name. It is too often an undigested group of unrelated facts, a mere calendaring of local events; when the first drug store was established (not why it was needed, not by whom it was established, not how it prospered or failed, not what it contributed to the community); who was the third mayor (not whether he was effective in what directions, his background, his contributions); who was pastor of the Congregational church when the town burned down. The preservation of such data is valuable, but this approach is strictly antiquarian.

Secondly "local" history is often romanticized. Folk myth and fairy tale abound in local history: all the first settlers were models of probity, industry, and decorum (which is possible but highly unlikely); the local veteran of the Civil War was a "general" (again highly unlikely); so-and-so's ancestor beat off an Indian attack single-handed and saved the settlement (when actually in a drunken stupor he had shot a single Indian coming to trade with the villagers, and in so doing nearly called down on the village a retaliatory massacre); the wine maker, who had imported to work his vineyards a colony of Italian families whose descendants presently are leaders in almost every form of activity in the town, was a benevolent, paternalistic boss who did everything for his workers (when actually he charged them high rents for their quarters, sold them food at the company's store at high profits, paid them very low wages, forced their children into the fields at the age of eight, offered no schooling, and held the immigrant families in a condition close to indentured servitude). Such gilding of lilies is common in old-style local history.

The term "localized" history has been adopted to indicate something quite different: sophisticated, realistic, soundly researched, factual, interpretive history of community, county, or region; or of components like local businesses, individual churches, schools, colleges, museums; or studies of less-than-nationally-significant figures whose contributions were primarily to the localized area. This is not antiquarian, it is not provincial, it is not romanticized.

There are almost no textbooks. Some good texts are coming into print at the state level, but few commercial publishers can afford to bring out a community history. Usually the teacher is not a native of the community and has been taught to teach from texts—always a convenient crutch. But there is no text—no nice, neat package of history for your particular community. So much the better. You can start from scratch, without preconceptions, without prejudices, without your work spoiled for you by others. Indeed not having a textbook on the history of the community offers a distinct educational advantage. It opens the way for all sorts of learning situations and participation projects at all levels. The students will enjoy the chance to find out for themselves. The experience can be completely different from anything else in the curriculum, and fresh, stimulating, intellectually invigorating.

Background material, if you feel you have to have it, can be found in a number of places (see pages 29ff). But even the teacher doesn't have to know the history of the community to guide effective class work in community history. It's not the same as having to know medieval history or Oriental history before you teach a class. You are already familiar at least with the outlines of American history and American government. Localized history is just the infinitely varied example of the national generalization, with, as I have suggested, lots of surprises and lots of variants.

It cannot be repeated too often that local materials offer challenges for students of every age and of every degree of sophistication. It is just as useful for high school offerings in American history, or special-credit projects, or for advanced-credit courses in American government or problems of American democracy as it is for the third or fourth grade.

# 2

## Research in Community Resources

THE famed second edition of *Webster's New International Dictionary* defines research as a "critical and exhaustive investigation . . . having for its aim the discovery of new facts and their correct interpretation, the revision of accepted conclusions . . . in the light of newly discovered facts." The *Oxford English Dictionary* records a simple definition dating back to 1694: "investigation, inquiry into things."

Investigations or inquiries into "things" start in earliest childhood as the baby, wondrous-eyed, investigates his crib, his mother, his clothes, himself. He reaches another state with the first "why." He reaches a third stage with a mastery of reading and the acquired ability to "look things up." He reaches a final stage with the ability for "critical and exhaustive investigation," "correct interpretation," and "the revision of accepted conclusions."

Philip Jordan, in *The Nature and Practice of State and Local History*, points out at what an early age research in localized history can begin. He suggests the kind of rudimentary initial report a third-grader might submit on the history of his school building, and how this could lead to attempts to locate some of the bricklayers who built the school, one of whom may help locate the brickyard where the bricks were made. It is now the site of a filling station, and thus, Jordan points out, "the lesson of change has been learned in a small way."[1] A search in the local newspaper turns up the obituary of the owner of the brickyard, a trip to the cemetery reveals his grave in the section for Civil War veterans. So one thing leads to another, and very early in the curriculum, simple research projects open up wide vistas in the hands of the imaginative teacher.

## Topics in Localized History

Topics are available in almost infinite variety. Any topic can be explored for a particular period in the community's development, or for the entire history

[1] Philip Jordan, *The Nature and Practice of State and Local History* (Washington, D.C., 1958) , p. 19.

of the locality, or by a particular phase of the topic. Let's look quickly at some of the possibilities.

## THE PEOPLE

Start with the people. What is the population of the community today? How do you know? Is the population growing? Has it grown steadily since the town was first settled? Why? Or have there been periods when the population receded? If so, why? Indian massacres? Depopulation for a gold rush? Or free land farther west which seemed more attractive for farming? A plague? A disaster such as a series of floods or a major fire which drove many to seek new homes elsewhere? Better transportation facilities nearby which made a local industry move? More and better jobs in the next town? Has the community been steadily declining in population since a peak reached many years ago? Or did it decline for a while and then begin to grow again? What were the reasons?

Who were (and are) the people who came to live in the community? Where did they come from? Why? Not just the first settlers but the later immigrants, from Europe or Asia or Africa, or from Canada, or Mexico, or other parts of the United States. We don't usually call these last immigrants, but they literally have migrated to the community from somewhere else and can in many senses be considered immigrants (though not, as they sometimes are, as foreigners!). The general pattern of language, law, and custom is English in origin, because the nucleus of the future nation was the relatively heavily settled English colonies along the Eastern seaboard. But we have inherited place names and descendants of traders from the smaller and more scattered French trading posts and forts in the midwest that were ceded to Great Britain in 1763, and Louisiana law is still based on the Napoleonic code. The Spanish settlements in Florida, the Gulf coast, and the Southwest have left their traces in place names, architecture, forts, missions, land patterns, and first families. If the community was settled by New Englanders, Yankee influence is probably still visible in the town plan (with a common), the architecture of the first substantial houses, and perhaps in an annual town meeting. If it was settled by Southerners, there are apt to be visible differences in the town plan and the architecture; there is apt to be government by commission, a different use of the grand jury. And if the community was either initially settled or later heavily populated by Poles, or Italians, or Greeks, or Germans, or Chinese, or others, it is almost certain to bear the marks to any sensitive or discerning eye.

Communities heavily populated by people from abroad are particularly worth study in a variety of special ways. What did these people contribute that made their communities different? Did the immigrant groups organize their own social groups? Did they start benevolent societies to give each other some rudimentary protection (burial insurance, for instance) and security in this strange land? What particular handicaps did they face? What sort of jobs did most of the newcomers hold? Probably clannish at first in the new country, how and how soon did they begin to break down barriers and enter political, social, and economic life on terms of equality with the native-born Americans? What special contributions did they bring, like the Czech family compact which provided genuine social security for the older generation while giving the middle-aged an opportunity to take over management of farm or shop while in their prime? Or the Polish New Year's communion in which the head of the family breaks a special large communion wafer with each member of his family, as each in turn wishes the rest the best of new years?

Did they bring special national dishes, such as pizza and spaghetti, or sweet-and-sour pork and bean sprouts, bagels and blintzes, pasties and meat pies, lutefisk and gefultefish? When did these dishes begin to make their way into the diet of the general community? (Newspaper ads will be one clue.) Did they bring with them certain folk dances which are now danced widely in the community? Or certain national holidays or religious festivals? One thinks of the Belgian kermiss, the German schützenfest, the Swiss kilby, the Italian celebration of the Feast of Our Lady of Mt. Carmel, the Indian pow-wow, the Welsh eisteddfod, and a hundred others. Are these still part of the community life? Why? or why not?

A different approach, equally rewarding, would be to investigate the national origins of accepted parts of the community culture like the Christmas tree (the German tannenbaum), the Yule log (English), rosemaling (Norwegian), yodeling (Swiss), mistletoe (French), the kindergarten (German and Swiss), dragon kites (Chinese), or talk of gremlins and little people (Irish).

## THE BEGINNINGS

Why did the early settlers settle where they did? Did they choose a hill or a level area? Was it at the mouth of a river, on a good harbor, or at the meeting place of two roads? How has the location influenced the development of the community? Was it subject to flood? Were there swamps nearby from which mosquitoes could spread ague and fever a century ago, or malaria? Was the soil sandy, rocky, loamy? Was the climate cold or warm, dry or moist, subject to major seasonal variations? Was there an easily accessible water supply? Is the original water supply still adequate? Were there natural resources of any significant kind: iron, coal, oil, gold, uranium? Did the first settlers know of these resources, or were they discovered later? What effect did these resources have on the development of the community, on the number and origins of the people who came there to live, on the development of transportation facilities, on banking deposits, on taxes and civic improvements, on the schools?

How did these people earn a living? Is it a farming community? Or was it once? What sort of farming? Different kinds of farming at different periods? Subsistence farming to start with, enough to keep the pioneer household going? Or specialization in wheat, or cotton, or vines, or rice, or indigo, potatoes, peanuts, or mushrooms? Or timber harvesting? Or combinations of several of these? Agriculture and cattle-raising can be studied crop by crop and period by period. They can be studied in terms of change of product (from one crop to another), or in changes of productivity and farm techniques (such as intensive cultivation, or irrigation, or chemical fertilization, or improved seed, or contour plowing, for instance). They can be studied in relation to transportation (the opening of avenues of trade by which to dispose of surplus production is the essential ingredient in evolving from subsistence farming to market farming); or in relation to immigration (certain national groups will bring native crops and native procedures with them); or in relation to government and governmental policy (national price-supports have local ramifications, as do soil banks, acreage retirement, production quotas, etc.).

## THE TOWN

Every reasonably heavily settled rural area quickly developed a center, a town where basic services were available. The community may have started as a single cabin where a pioneer family hewed its living out of a forest, girdling the trees, planting foodstuffs hopefully sufficient to last out the year; or it may have started around a shelter built from the sod of the prairie; or around a post established by the English, or the French, or the Spanish, or the Russians, or the U.S. government for trade with the Indians. Or it may have been a frontier fort strategically placed to defend routes of trade or migration, to affirm a colonial nation's claim to an area, or later to protect nearby settlers from Indian depredations. Often the town grew up around the gristmill, the sawmill, the smithy, perhaps the tannery or a brick factory; at a crossroads, or at a point on river or lakeshore where boats could tie up conveniently and safely. It might be a day's wagon haul or more from the farthest farm it served. Here were the church, the school, the doctor, perhaps a few shops. Here, once the population became large enough to support them and they could stop traveling from farm to farm, the cobbler, the cooper, the wheelwright, and other early servicemen settled down. Then came still better transportation, first the railroad and much later the automobile and truck, using the farm-to-market road. Some towns grew. Services became more specialized. There were more stores of more types. The more easily and rapidly people could travel (and goods could be moved), the more major centers tended to rise, at greater distances from the individual farm or home, with more and more specialized services to offer for a fee. Other towns lost out in the competition. They might still boast a mill and a store and a church, but most of the trade went to the larger community where more services and more specialties were available. Yet life there was more even-paced and living more enjoyable. Which kind of community do you live in?

## BUSINESS AND INDUSTRY

The rise of the town offered the people of the community many different ways to earn their living, and it offers us an almost unlimited supply of topics to investigate. Whatever has been or is represented in the community in the way of business and industry has a history. A small business, a small department store, a shoe or clothing store, a grocery or a market, or a hardware store, is worth study; and the changes that have taken place in size, in profits, in items sold (reflecting changing community needs and taste), in market area served—the story of the men who made that store what it is today, what it replaced, or why it came into existence when it did, what function and timeliness it had when established—will bring about an understanding of another facet of the local story and the workings of the American economy.

Industry may be represented at a given period by anything from a blacksmithy to a huge steel plant or a tremendous automated factory. It may be extractive (a mine, a gas or oil or salt well, a peat bog, a marsh yielding marsh grass). It may be a manufactory, changing raw materials into totally different goods. It may be a service industry, distributing a certain kind or kinds of products, or providing for their maintenance and repair (a gasoline station, a television repair shop, a barber shop, or a huge trucking or shipping concern). It may be owned by a single man, or by a family, or by partners, or by a corporation the stock of which may be widely held and publicly traded on the stock exchange or entirely held within a small group of the founders or a single family. It may be a small shop making just one type of product, or it may be a huge corporation which with widely diversified holdings makes widely diversified products. Whatever business and industry is locally represented will lead you not only through various aspects of the community's history, but into wider and wider horizons and insights into the history and economy of the nation and the world.

## TRADE AND COMMUNICATION

Similarly, the local transportation situation will lead you to the heart of the economy. By land, sea, air, or underground; by foot, horseback, coach, buggy, wagon, truck, bus, or auto; by canoe, sail, or steam; by wood-burner, steam, or diesel; by trolley or inter-urban; by biplane or jet, man and his goods have been moved. And the community and its population and its economy change as its transportation changes. So one can study the changes in the forms of local transportation and the resulting changes in the life of the community. Or one can study a single form of transportation and its impact on the community, the jobs it created directly, the other jobs it created indirectly, the men who established it, the men who put up the money to make it possible. Again, insights and understanding result.

And so for the other forms of communication: the mail, the telegraph, the telephone, the radio (as used for communication, not entertainment), and what they have meant to the conduct of business and government, and so to the individual community.

Radio for entertainment and television are also industries, employing people directly and creating other jobs such as those in advertising agencies, radio and TV sales, and repair shops. Here is another avenue for seeing how things happen and how the wheels go around in our society and economy.

What did people pay for what they bought? Any prices of yesterday may seem very cheap indeed considering comparable prices today. But the obverse of the coin is what people were paid for their labor, for the produce of their ranch or mine or shop, for their services. Here the range is from very simple basic economics to very sophisticated economics, from very simple history to very complex history. Here is understanding of farm unrest at various periods of our history, here is background for the rise of organized labor, here is material for understanding what makes an economy grow or stagnate in a town—or a nation, or a civilization.

## LABOR

And what of organized labor in your community? The story is very different in New York City or Kohler, Wisconsin; in Birmingham, Alabama, or Centralia, Washington What unions are represented in your community? How long has each local been established? Each central body? How far back does the history of each international go? Why and under what circumstances did labor organize in your community? What has organized labor done in your community? What has it secured for its members in wages and fringe benefits? What has it done for the community in fields outside its own special jurisdiction, such as education, medical care, social work? Has it been active in politics? And if you want a really sophisticated topic to investigate, look into the effects of the successes of organized labor on the prices and therefore the markets for the products of local industry and on the welfare of the industry. Or look into what the union's attitude is toward automation in its industry.

## THE PROFESSIONS

Still other members of the community, for most of its history, will have earned their living through practicing a profession: law, medicine, education, theology. How many lawyers have there been in your community at various times in the past? What kinds of law have they practiced? What does this tell you about the needs of the community at that time? About its stage of development? How many churches or synagogues or mosques does the community have? When was each established? What does this tell you about the history of the community, the people who settled there at different periods? And what does the architecture of these religious buildings tell you about the development of the community, its taste, its wealth?

## EDUCATION

How about the schools: not just the number of buildings or the number of pupils (though both are highly significant), but the changes in the type of building and the facilities of schools of different periods, the changes in the curriculum, the changes in the hours of instruction, the changes in the minimum age to which one must attend school? All these tell you a lot about the development of the community and of the nation. Are there church schools in your community? Or other private schools ("academies" or preparatory schools)? How about a comparative study of their enrollment, their curricula, their histories, their role in the community's educational picture?

## THE ARTS AND CRAFTS

There may have been some important craftsmen in your community: a cabinet-maker whose work is not as famous as that of Duncan Phyfe, but who had genuine competence and whose tables and chairs and desks and dressers— where recognized—command local attention; or a glass-blower who moved from Bohemia or Italy and plied his craft in your town, alternating his bread-and-butter pieces with some highly decorative and lovely pitchers and paper-weights; or a blacksmith with the time and the talent to turn out some decorative iron work that ranks among the best; or a potter whose ceramics still command premium prices. The stories of these men will cast significant light on the position the craftsman held in our society and economy, chiefly in earlier days.

So will the stories of the local artists, the painters, sculptors, and musicians, the town has produced. Perhaps they moved away. Why? Perhaps they stayed on, or at least maintained a home base in your community. Which they did will tell you something significant about your community. Most communities have had a writer or two in their history, a poet, a novelist, a short-story writer. And some communities have produced theatrical stars, circus performers, and professional athletes who excelled in baseball, basketball, football, boxing, or wrestling. What these people did in relation to your community; whether they stayed there or moved away; what they did locally—if they stayed—in their off-seasons will furnish insights as to the kind of people they were and the kind of community yours was when they lived there.

## GOVERNMENT

How about government? How have changing forms and functions of local government reflected the changing needs of the period? Does the county board or the board of supervisors, or the common council, or the board of aldermen have the same functions it did fifty (or a hundred) years ago? If not, what are the differences? Names sometimes remain the same while functions change. How has the changing impact of county, state, and federal government affected the local scene? In appropriate areas, one can study the special problems of suburban government, the moves for regional consolidation or cooperation, and the sources and reason for resistance. The evolution of the right to vote, from limited white male suffrage to universal adult suffrage, offers challenging possibilities. The political organization or machine and the changes in that organization, its effectiveness and its morality, are clearly visible at the local level. So too are its relationships to the county organization, to the state organization, and to the national party. So are the workings, where they exist or have existed, of the initiative, referendum, and recall and the short ballot. Again one can start with the simplest and most elemental materials at a very early age. Or one can explore the most sophisticated areas in the final years of high school.

## RECREATION

Finally, how about recreation? How has the community amused itself? With active or spectator sports? With turkey shoots and barn-raisings or with movies and television? With spelling bees and square dances or scrimshaw and crossword puzzles? With reading or with picture puzzles? Americans are said to be great joiners; they join all sorts of organizations, many of which do all sorts of jobs in the community's service. We call this "volunteerism." What sort of organizations (Masons and Knights of Columbus, womens' clubs, Salvation Army and Volunteers of America, Rotary and Kiwanis and Lions, Elks and Moose and Woodmen, and— especially earlier—Knights Templar, Knights of Pythias, Knights of Labor, Grangers) do you have and have you had in your community? What good works have they performed and are they performing? What have they contributed? The way man spends his leisure time, and has spent it in past generations, tells us much of the people, much of the period, much of the community.

So whatever exists or has existed in your community, wherever you choose to poke and explore, you will find some of the keys to understanding not only what has made the community but what has made America what it is today. You achieve with particular clarity some of that perspective, balance, insight, and wisdom that come from the study of history because you are using materials, situations, institutions, things that are already familiar to you; they are part of your home environment, your own neighborhood, your local community.

## Organizing Research Programs

There are two major ways of organizing classes to do research. The traditional way is to assign a topic to each student, let him work it up, put it in writing, and present it—preferably to the whole class. This requires a good deal of individualized supervision and suggestion from the teacher, who may be considerably handicapped in such an approach by not being himself an authority on community history. It can be used, it can be effective, but it is hard. It is particularly recommended for the superior student who, for instance, could be given an assignment in what would amount to independent research in community history.

More productive in most circumstances is the cooperative research project in which the entire class pools its talents and resources in a common project. Perhaps a committee of students, perhaps the whole class (with the help of the teacher) maps out the topic to be investigated and explored. The group develops the research plan, considers likely resources, and decides who should gather certain data, where to look for certain information, who should be interviewed, where certain illustrative objects could be sought. Then each student takes his agreed assignment. At subsequent meetings, each reports his findings. Particularly he emphasizes his frustrations: what he could not find out, his roadblocks, his failures. His classmates and the teacher pool suggestions, and off the student goes to try again, perhaps learning how and where to find certain data, perhaps learning that in research as in many other things the first try is not always successful, perhaps learning that answers can be found if you look long enough and hard enough and in the right places, perhaps achieving that wonderful flash of enlightenment when two pieces of the puzzle fit together and an insight is born. Formal research of this sort can be supplemented very usefully and helpfully by various field trips and visits to the class by people in one occupation or another. Suggestions for such events appear in the next chapter.

After a number of sessions, the topic will be about exhausted for a given age level, and it is then time to write up the class findings.

## The Sources of Localized History

What are the sources of localized history? History is where you find it. Localized history is everywhere, and so are its sources.

Background knowledge, if wanted, can usually be found at least in part in several different places. Most states have been the subject of published volumes of state history—sometimes a single volume, sometimes a multi-volume set. The index and chapter headings will be helpful in guiding you to pertinent material. Most counties have at least one printed history, often dating from the latter part of the nineteenth century. These, for the most part, are the so-called "mug books," containing a biographical section for which people prepared their own sketches and paid for their inclusion. An extra fee entitled one to one's picture. The biographies are a bit uncritical since each is written by the biographee. The county histories themselves are of widely different caliber. A few are very good, most are quite poor. But good and bad alike will give you some help on a rudimentary background of the history of your community. Many cities, towns, and villages, companies, colleges, and churches have also had their histories written and published. They will be helpful, but may leave unanswered questions of the type you will be exploring. Many local histories have been published, often serially in the local newspaper. The school, or certainly the public library, will have a copy of or at least a reference to the issues of the newspapers in which these articles appeared. The history of many localities has been written, but not published. These unpublished manuscripts may be found in the public library or the local historical society. Published or unpublished, use these materials only for guidance, not as authorities. They are apt to be filled with the folk-myth and romantic nonsense on which we have already commented (p. 16). They are apt to be inadequately researched. They are apt to miss both the wider implications and the real significance of what they record. They are guides, not gospel.

Many newspapers run, or have run, columns on what happened in the community ten or twenty-five or fifty years ago. These usually carry only a sentence per event, and some events are obviously more important than others. But if they record local, as distinct from national or international, events, they are suggestive. The paper also has probably run at several different periods historical accounts or articles which will be useful.

In addition, the local newspaper is the diary of the community, recording events as they take place and in considerable detail. What is recorded tends to be simple and dramatic: the coming of the railroad, the opening of a new plant, a fire or flood, an election, the appearance of a national figure in town, the opening of a new bridge, the high school commencement, the repaving of Second Avenue. Advertisements give indication of price levels. Weather forecasts may record a prolonged drought. Job columns indicate salary levels. Legal notices may be important. The local paper seldom does the reflective, background, summary kind of article which is so very useful to the historian, but a lot of raw material lies in every local newspaper.

Government documents can be important sources. Federal and state studies often contain data (economic, geological, statistical, sociological) of significance to your own community; your librarian will be helpful in identifying those of use to you on any particular project. Local ordinances are usually printed when passed (sometimes only in the newspapers). Many official local reports are printed. Particularly helpful, for recent years, are the annual reports of the superintendent of schools (more and more of which are being published each year as school budgets face more intense public surveillance), and the presentations outlining the major features of the community budget.

The more detailed original (manuscript) records in the several major community offices will be even more useful. Land deeds, in the office of the Registrar of Deeds, trace the title to a given piece of property and list the consecutive owners of record of a given tract of land from the beginning of valid title. Tax rolls on a given piece of property are a good index as to when a building first improved the property, or when the initial hut was replaced by a clapboard mansion or a business block. The City Treasurer's office (by whatever title it is known) will have a fascinating picture of the evolution of the community's finances and a detailed record of what the taxpayers' money has been spent for year by year by year. The street department can tell you when Main Street was paved, what sorts of pavement (timber, timber block, corduroy, gravel, cobblestone, brick, macadam, concrete, bituminous asphalt, etc.) have been used consecutively and probably on what streets and will give you all sorts of information as to the advantages and disadvantages of different types of pavement. The water department can tell you when water pipes and sewers were installed in different parts of the community and can help on the history of sewage treatment and disposal. The health department can give you many vital statistics: the records of births and deaths, morbidity rates, and so forth. And the board of education can help you greatly with the history of your school and the school system and curriculum of the community.

The broadsides advertising for a runaway slave, a substitute for a man drafted for the Union forces, a reduced steamship fare, a special lecture at the opera house, the coming of a circus, or the latest attraction at the nickelodeon may be just what is needed to fill in a particular bit of information. Files are apt to be found at the local library and the historical society.

The magazine article on some event or person of more than local interest may be helpful. So may the printed diary, the printed letter or letters, the memoirs of a local leader, political, industrial, or social. So will be the program of the local event, the dedication, the centennial observance of a local church or the library or the town itself, and the brochures or books printed in connection with such events. Or the program of the local theater or lecture or art show or dance or banquet. Or some of the promotional material prepared for the Chamber of Commerce. Check with the library and historical society.

Biographical sketches of prominent figures will appear in the *Dictionary of American Biography, Appleton's Cyclopedia of American Biography, Who Was Who in America, Who's Who in America* and its regional children like

*Who's Who in the East,* the *Directory of American Scholars,* the whole shelf of who's who type volumes: *Who's Who in Music, Who's Who in American Jewry,* and so on. Professional directories like the *Martindale-Hubbell Law Directory* or P. E. Mohr, *American Medical Directory* may be of limited use. At least two states, Texas *(Handbook of Texas History)* and Wisconsin *(Dictionary of Wisconsin Biography),* have issued volumes including biographical sketches of men and women prominent in the history of these states. Obituaries and other articles in the newspapers when someone dies are of help. So, too, are the resolutions adopted by the organization or organizations to which a person belonged when he or she dies. So, too, are the self-composed biographical sketches in the county histories already referred to, *if* you remember that the person wrote the sketch about himself and paid for its insertion in the book.

Many basic statistics are obtainable from the published federal census, taken at the beginning of each new decade. Many more are obtainable in the several state censuses taken in many states for many years in the middle of each decade. For localized statistics, the manuscript censuses, available from the National Archives on microfilm through 1870, are most useful. Here you can find not just the number of people in the community, but the occupation of each, the number of persons in the family, their age and sex. The census also shows the number of industrial establishments, from potash producers or munitions makers in earlier days to automobile plants and sugar refineries today, with the number of employees. The published census statistics give useful summaries. Most newspapers give local summaries when the census appears. City directories, published regularly (every year in many cases), list heads of families and businesses with street address and occupation and may be more readily available.

There will be many handwritten or typed (not printed) sources: the reminiscences of a citizen, an autobiography, a diary, a file of letters, the ledgers and journals of a store or an industry, the minutes of an official body such as the Common Council or of a literary society or a church auxiliary.

Court records, particularly the exhibits, can be extraordinarily revealing of ways of life, of prices and business methods, of social problems in the community at various stages of its history. Unfortunately such materials are not readily usable unless the local county courthouse has a (probably elderly) keeper of the records who really knows what is in his files and how to find it, or there is some member of the bar who has studied the history of the local court. Wills, on file in the probate court, are indicative of what sorts and amounts of property a person in a certain economic and social position (ascertainable elsewhere) was apt to have at any particular period.

There will be oral sources: the people who participated in some movement or event, or who have excellent memories of what happened in the town in other years in politics, or in business, or in other areas. Human memory is highly fallible, and memories must be checked against records. But the memory of participants is often the best clue as to why something was done or attempted when it was, what the motives of various people were in certain situations. If the student interviews a citizen, he should take careful notes; his own memory may be quite fallible. If a tape recording is made, it should be made by someone who already knows a good deal about the topic under discussion so that the person being interviewed can be kept on the track and so that questionable data can be challenged at the time and further explanation obtained.

In almost every community there are one or more people who have made a hobby of knowing the history of the community. Usually they are more than willing to share their knowledge with school children, and usually they are willing to have questions asked as to their sources: not just what they know but how they happen to know it. The local historical society or the local librarian can usually identify such people for you.

There will be physical remains: the photograph, the print, the tool, the forge, the painting, the implement, the vessel, the vehicle, the building, the ruin, the site, the telegraph key, the fire engine, the lottery wheel for the Civil War draft, the abandoned right-of-way, the ditch of the old canal, the mine head and tailings, the sluice and the millstone, the earthworks, the dentist's turnkey, the leech box.

For the more advanced student, this is an appropriate time to introduce the difference between primary and secondary sources: the *primary* source being an original source—a letter, a diary, an account book, a minute book, a personal reminiscence, an unretouched photograph; the *secondary* source being a second-hand, reconstructed account of what happened: a newspaper, a magazine article, a book (other than one of reminiscences), a sketch, print, or painting made after an event.

Between things you can read, things you can see, and people of whom you can ask questions, there are may sources of localized history readily at hand. A little looking, a little probing, will yield a lot.

## *Writing and Publishing Localized History*

The class's work should be summarized in writing, as an exercise in composition, in organizing material, and in putting it into logical, cohesive, intelligent, and intelligible form.

After the class and the teacher are convinced that the subject has been about exhausted for them, it is time to start writing. The best writer may be asked to prepare a draft, or each student may write up his or her part of the research. A draft is put together and discussed by the class in a sort of junior seminar. Perhaps additional drafts are written and discussed.

This is a good point at which to introduce, in connection with the class discussion of evidence, the concepts of documentation, the use of footnotes (which will be very useful for the student going on to college), and bibliography.[2] This is not just a mechanical or purely technical exercise. It is a hallmark of seriousness of purpose and effort. The earlier a student learns that he must be ready to cite his sources, substantiate his assertions, the better off he will be. I have seen rudimentary footnoting successfully introduced as early as the fifth grade. Obviously more can be expected at the senior high school level, but an early start is highly desirable.

The best of what is written should be published—partly as a reward, a prestigious public recognition, of the students' work; partly as a contribution to knowledge of the history of the community, precious little of which may be in print. And there are more outlets available in the average community than one might suppose.

First, there is the school newspaper. Second, there is in many states today a statewide magazine for junior historians, sponsored by the state historical society or department. Almost all of these magazines print the best essays prepared by school students who are themselves junior historians (see chapter 6).

Third, if the project has been sufficiently ambitious and enough material is produced, there is a good possibility of publishing it as a book or booklet. This costs money, but there are many ways to raise the necessary funds, from cookie sales to car-washes—all the many means of fund-raising with which the student today is well acquainted. There is also a good chance that such a book or booklet will be self-sufficient, that enough people will buy copies to pay for the costs of printing and binding. A local printer may give a good price and a good student sales organization ought to be able to dispose of the stock at a reasonable price, perhaps even turn a modest profit. Or a local civic club, a patriotic society, or a local business firm may underwrite the venture. The circumstances will vary from one community to another, but publication in book form should not be rejected as impossible without full investigation.[3]

A fourth possibility is the local historical society, which probably does not publish many books but might be sufficiently intrigued by the origin of this particular manuscript to be willing to assume the costs of its publication and the responsibility for marketing it.

Fifth, there is the local newspaper. Unquestionably there is wide reader interest in local history, not only in the locality itself but among former residents.

---

[2] Simple rules of footnoting can be found in L. Appel, *Bibliographical Citations in the Social Sciences and the Humanities* (Madison, Wisc., 1949), a copy of which *should* be in your school library if it is not.

[3] A notable example is Margaret S. Carter (comp.), *New Diggings is an Old Diggings*, prepared by a group of rural school children in New Diggings, Wisc., under the supervision of Mrs. Carter, their teacher, and published at New Diggings, 1948, 111 pp.

One weekly newspaper which began to run a full page of local history once a month rapidly gained a substantial circulation among former residents who had retired to California.[4] Add the special interest adults have in young people and their work, and you have a special feature that will interest many newspaper editors.

Then there is the local radio station, always looking for material of special local interest. Again the particular appeal of the younger generation adds the fillip that might get them air time that the adult historical society might be unable to command. Many stations are glad to have a local show with a youthful cast; they know the wide adult appeal of such programs. And the chance to appear on radio is an additional experience for the students. Dissemination by air does not give the permanency of record that print in book form or in the newspapers offers, but it does get the material across at least temporarily to a considerable audience. Also most stations produce their scripts by mimeograph or an offset process, and copies of the scripts can be secured for the school and libraries.

If all else fails, the school mimeograph machine or the typing department can turn out a number of copies for the school and local libraries and perhaps for sale to interested people.

The point is that the best work done in the school should not be junked. It should be given long life through publication in one form or another. And that which is not good enough to publish can well be filed in the school library to help the next group which tackles the subject to avoid duplicating what you have already done.

---

[4] *Sawyer County Gazette,* Hayward, Wisc., which for several years ran a monthly one-page "Sawyer County Historical Review" prepared by the members of the county historical society.

# 3

*Field Trips*

FIELD trips are no novelty in most schools. But the full utilization of such resources for the study of the community, either for its own sake or to illustrate the larger story of American development, is seldom achieved. There is no limit to the number and type of field trips which can be taken profitably by a class of any grade level and any degree of sophistication. The following suggestions are limited to the field of community history: political, economic, social, and intellectual.

## The Museum

Museums are said to be opening in this country at the rate of two a week. There is almost certainly a historical museum within bus range of your school. It may be a separate historical museum, or it may be the museum of the local (or county or state) historical society. It will undoubtedly have exhibits of interest to the student of the history of the community—either directly and specifically in the local historical museum or society, or having an obvious bearing on what happened in your community in terms of wider developments in the county or state. Not all historical museums are so organized, and not all historical societies have museums of their own. But this is a good place to start lining up field trips. Contact the local, county, and state historical societies—if they have museum exhibits—and the separate historical museums. Ask what they are exhibiting, see how this fits the pattern of your course, and then decide whether or not to take the class. If you decide to go, and can possibly do so, go first by yourself. Get acquainted with the staff member at the society or museum who takes care of school groups. See what the exhibits cover, so that the class can do the most effective possible preparatory work and therefore get the most out of what must necessarily be a short visit. What do you want to be sure the students see? What will they find most provocative and stimulating? Can you tie the visit not only to history but, perhaps, to the sciences through the display on the local inventor, or on the special properties of the iron lode in the area, or of the local clay on which the ceramic industry is based? If you can't first go by yourself, most museums today have literature for the teacher, indicating what is to be seen and suggesting preparatory studies for the class.

Be sure to make advance arrangements with the society or museum for your visit. Find out about eating facilities and rest rooms. Many local historical societies open their museums only at certain hours or only by appointment. Many larger ones are swamped with visitors and can do an effective job with school groups only if their visits are scheduled well ahead of time. Fit your visit to the society or museum to the development of the work in your course—another reason why you must know in advance what is on exhibit in a given society or museum. And be sure to follow up the visit with class discussions and assessments of the learning experience. Perhaps a discussion of what makes a good museum display will be useful, not only in preparing displays for your own school museum (see chapter 4) but in developing the students' critical sense in a nonliterary field.

## *The Historic Site*

Historic sites can have great educational impact. These are the places where history happened. Few Americans can visit Appomattox, or Sutter's Mill, or Yorktown, or Promontory Point, or Emigration Canyon, or Cumberland Gap, or Harpers Ferry, or Los Alamos, without a sense of closeness to something vital and important in the making of America. There are two kinds of sites: (1) "bare" sites, where about all there is to see is the lay of the land; and (2) sites with structures or buildings, restored or reconstructed. The former are the less satisfactory, though to see Bunker Hill or Little Round Top or Blennerhassett's Island is surely to have a new sense of being close to history. But a Williamsburg, a Sturbridge, a Dearborn or a Salem, a Mission San Juan Capistrano or the synagogue at Truro, Ford's Theatre in Washington or the Silver Dollar at Virginia City, New Salem, Ill., or Fort Snelling, Minn., the Alamo or Independence Hall, give a deeply moving sense of the immediacy and intimacy of the past. This is where history comes alive. So does our sense of debt to those on whose shoulders we stand.

"Bare" sites may have an explanatory marker but little else, though most of those in the National Park Service's jurisdiction are equipped with reception areas where the story of the site is told by guides or displays or both. This model is being followed as finances permit in the states and at many privately owned sites. But the sites with buildings in almost all instances have guides and displays, cater to visitors, welcome school groups. Again tie your visit to the appropriate point in your study. Again contact the site in advance, schedule your visit to the mutual convenience of class and site, get any advance literature that may be available, study before the visit, discuss and assess after the trip.

During the term, at the time when it best fits the curriculum, visit as many places where significant things are happening as possible. If it is a seasonal activity, such as any kind of farming, the curriculum schedule has to yield to the seasonal visibility of the activity. But normally, for example, the time to visit the railroad is when you are talking about the railroads and their role in the national economy; the time to visit the oil refinery is when you are talking about oil and its many roles and uses.

Trips to these places where things are happening today—as distinct from museums and historic sites which perpetuate the things that happened yesterday —can be immensely rewarding. But caveats are very much in order:

(1) Too often such field trips are oriented only to the immediate present: what people do now, how the modern bakery turns out one thousand loaves an hour, how glass is made today, what the recreation department does during the year. Too little attention is given to illustrating the forces of change, to the history of baking or glass or recreation; to how these operations have changed right in your community, and what this has meant in terms of jobs, of productivity, of standards of living, of growing wealth and leisure, of greater specialization, and of the political, social, and economic problems that accompany change and are part of history too. Never overlook the opportunity to supplement on the site what you have learned in class about the history that has been made in the past. Find out all you can not just about what is going on today, but what has happened in the past, and the changes involved; about how those now working in a given field think and understand about what their predecessors accomplished, or tried to do.

(2) These field trips should not be confined, as they are in some school systems, to the lower grades. The meaning of a board of aldermen, a port of entry, or a steel plant is one thing at that level and quite another in senior high. Community materials are useful, stimulating, and provocative at all school ages and at all levels of sophistication.

What are some of the activities that should be visited?

# The Farm

In most parts of the country (including Manhattan Island) there is at least some farming within bussing distance. Visit a farm, preferably a large commercial farm. It may be a truck farm, specializing in products like celery, lettuce, cabbage, carrots, and other vegetables for the urban table. It may be primarily a tobacco farm, or a cotton plantation, or a rice plantation, or a fruit farm. Find out why the farmer grows what he does; climate will have a lot to do with it but not everything. What does he grow besides his main crop? Does he raise his own foodstuffs? Why, or why not? How much machinery does he use on the farm, and what did it cost? Or does he rent it? Or does he borrow it from the local coop? What sort of fertilizer does he use, and what does it cost him each year? Ask him how long he has farmed this particular land. What can he tell you about how farming and marketing practices have changed in those years? Is he raising the same crops now as when he started? If there have been changes, why? Where does he market his produce? Does he market it himself, or through an intermediary with whom he contracts before the planting season (or at crop time) for his entire crop? Where does his crop go: to a major market center, to a cigarette manufacturer, to a cannery or a freezing unit? What about governmental restrictions on the size of the crop he can produce, or the number of acres he can cultivate? Does the government in turn guarantee him a minimum price for his crop? What does he think of this?

The "farm" may be a dairy farm, which will have its own problems of animal care, refrigeration of a perishable product, marketing, and transportation that are quite different from those of the potato grower. Or it may be a cattle ranch, with other problems of protection of the range from over-grazing, of water supply, of animal health, and again of marketing and transportation, as well as the special color of the roundup and the cowboy. Or it may be a tree farm, where lumber is the main product and the forest is cropped with scientific care.

Try to understand how farming has changed and how complex it has become; how heavy the capital investment; how uncertain the prospects in a given year when weather, insects, or flood may ruin the crop, or bumper crops the market. See farming for what it is today, a major industry, with each farm run as a business. Ask what the farmers think is the minimum efficient unit in their branch of farming. See what they do in the off-season. And if you visit some small farms, find out how many farmers and their families have jobs in the city to tide them over even the summer months.

But look at farming the historical way, too. How many people listed themselves as "farmers" in the census a hundred years ago in your county? How many so list themselves now? What has been happening—to the number of farmers, to the number of farms, to the size of individual farms, to the productivity of an acre of ground, to the number of jobs demanded by the growing and harvesting of crops?

Remember that Manhattan Island north of Wall Street was once all farms and forests. What has happened to the land in your vicinity? What do the tract books at the Registry of Deeds (or the Sanborn insurance atlases, which also show the boundaries of properties and the location of buildings) show you about the changes in use in your community? Once we were a nation of small farmers. Now only a small fraction of our population works in agriculture. What has happened in your community and its neighborhood? The chances are that the changes have been dramatic, reflecting the changing nature of the story that is our history.

## *Transportation*

Visiting the railroad roundhouse or switch yard or repair shops has long been standard school fare in the earliest grades. But here the student should not just learn how a locomotive is turned around on the turntable and how trains are made up or dispersed in the switch yards. He should find out what the railroad transports out of the community, from its farms and factories, and how much this is worth; where the community's exports go and from where its imports come. Forget about the passengers, who are economically unimportant; concentrate on the freight. How about the history of this railroad? When did it reach the community? Is this a branch line or the main line? How does the amount of freight in and out of the community compare with the amount ten and twenty and fifty years ago? Talk to the freight agent. Has there been talk of discontinuing railroad service—freight as well as passenger—to your community? What has been the public response? Why? What are the main competitors of your local railroad: trucks, pipelines, air freight, water transportation? When did each become important? Do piggy-backs (truck bodies transported on flat cars) operate in your community? Have they been successful? Can a student project himself back to the days before trucks and pipelines and air freight, and begin to realize the vital importance of the railroads when water transportation (usually moving in a different direction from that of the railroad) was the only competition? Can he see why the government thought it worthwhile to subsidize with generous land grants the construction of the transcontinental routes? Can he understand the temptations of the railroad owners which led to demands for rate and other regulations which in turn contributed to the present deteriorating situation of the roads? Visit the local truckers' association offices. Get comparable statistics on the amount and kinds of freight hauled in and out of town by truck. Get comparable statistics on the costs per ton mile of truck and railroad transportation for comparable goods today and ten years ago. Find out how union regulations affect both railroads and truck operations. How do governmental regulations affect each?

Air transport is available somewhere near any community today. We may think of this as primarily a means for people to travel, but air mail has been with us since 1918 and air freight is growing rapidly. A visit to the airport, not just to the control tower to watch how planes are brought in or sent off, not just to find out about the latest radar equipment for traffic control and for landings and takeoffs in poor visibility, but to get the statistics on air freight, is very much in order. Again, what kinds of goods are shipped in and out of your community by air? What is the cost per ton mile? What are the advantages that are bringing more and more shippers to call on air freight? How long has this been going on? And what are the advantages favoring railroad and truck over air freight?

To complete the freight transportation picture, how about water transportation? What are its advantages? What types of goods are carried in and out of the community by water, if water transportation—by river, canal, lake, or ocean—is available? What are the costs per ton mile, etc.? If there is a sizable port facility nearby, by all means visit it and study modern loading techniques, whether by the traditional crane, or by belt conveyors, or by automated devices in use for bulk cargoes like coal, or iron, or oil, or wheat. Again find out about government regulations, about the role and impact of labor unions, about the part water transport plays in the economy of the community. What has been the relative importance of water transportation in the history of the community? Is more cargo transported in and out of your community by water today than ten, twenty-five, fifty, one hundred years ago? Absolutely more, or more relative to the total amount of goods hauled in and out of the community by all means combined? Changes in transportation patterns mean changes in job patterns. And changes in job patterns often involve political repercussions. What has been the story in your community?

If you add questions like the size of the local payroll of each of these major forms of transportation, the taxes they pay in the community, the special services they render the business community, and the shifts in relative importance between them, you will have a pretty good picture of the role transportation has played in the economic life of the locality, a pretty good understanding of how it has affected the growth and development of the locality and of its crucial importance in the continuing life of the community.

What you can do for the farm or for transportation, you can do in many other areas of great importance to the understanding of how our country (and community) got to be what it is, how it operates, what makes it tick.

## Stores and Restaurants

The department store, with its hundreds of different items and types of items coming from widely scattered sources, can be a fascinating study in the complexity of management's tasks of selecting, ordering, merchandising. The hardware store or the restaurant can be equally rewarding. Where does the stock—whether it be nails or tools or kitchen utensils in the hardware shop, or dresses or shoes or leather goods in the department store, or hamburger meat or soup or pies in the restaurant—come from? What is the trade area served? How many people are employed? What is the total payroll? What is the profit margin? What are the problems peculiar to this trade? What of regulations and taxes and unions? How has the store changed in types of goods it carries, in sources of supply, in market area, in its use of customer credit, charge accounts and installment buying, in sales techniques? Is it an independent store, a unit of a regional chain, or a unit of a national chain? If either of the latter, what differences do you notice—if any—in the prices and varieties of goods for sale? And what are the constraints on the freedom of decision of the manager of such a store? Talk to him and find out. How "free" is the owner or manager of *any* store to make decisions? What are the constraints operating on *his* freedom of decision?

## The Factory

The manufacturing plant is well worth a visit. Don't go just to see how a stove, or an automobile, or a plastic bag, or a tin can, or whatever is made there is made. Find out how many cans are made a year, where they are shipped, who uses them, what the competition is, how many people are employed, whether work is seasonal or steady, what the payroll and taxes are, etc., etc., etc. Is the factory making the same articles it made when it was first built? If so, is it making them in the same way? How old is this factory? Has it been added to, or is it just the way it was when it was built? If there have been changes, what are they—in machinery, in techniques, in safety, in loading, in man-hours of labor needed to produce a single unit of its product, in wages, in price of the product? What do these changes signify? What have they meant to the company, to the employees, to the consumer, to the public?

## The Power Plant

Visit the power plant. Is it operated by water power, coal, powdered coal under forced draft, oil, or atomic power? If by water power, how old is the dam? What did it cost? How was the cost financed? What lay in the valley behind the dam? If by coal or oil, how is it brought to the plant? From where? What is the cost of producing a kilowatt-hour of electricity? What is the sales price? Are there different rates for small and large users? Why? Who are the major users besides the home owners? Is this particular utility publicly owned or privately owned? Is it subject to any particular local, or state, or federal regulation? Why? Since when? How wide an area does it serve? How is it combatting voltage loss in transmission? The correlation between manufacturing and available power is obvious and great. What effect has this plant had on manufacturing in its service area? What do the statistics show?

## The Mine

How about the nearby mine, whether for coal or oil or gas or salt or iron or uranium? When was it opened? How many people are employed? What is the payroll? What are the taxes? Where does the product go? Has employment been steady? If not, why not, and with what effects locally? What are the estimated local reserves for the future? What is the history of the mine? What government and union regulations affect its operation?

## The Resort

Or the resort. Where do its clients come from? What do they spend in the community (this has to be an educated "guestimate") while at the resort? Is this a seasonal resort? What do the people who are employed there do in the off-season? How long has this resort existed? Does it represent a form of recreation which became popular only recently, or does its interest for the public go well back into history? If the latter, has the nature of its clientele (social, economic, cultural status) changed over the years? What effects have such changes had on the community?

## The Bank

Another area of great potential for a field trip is the local bank. Here is one of the highly sophisticated and central institutions of our economy. There is much to see here besides money-sorting machines, vaults with intricate timing mechanisms, microfilm cameras photographing in miniature each check cashed each day, accounting machines, perhaps cameras focussed on each cage to photograph everyone who approaches just in case he might be bent on robbery. The big thing to see in a bank is the lines of people walking up to the counters: the messenger from the store depositing the hundreds of checks received that day from customers paying for goods the store brought in from all over the world; the elderly widow cashing her social security check to pay her rent and buy some groceries; the armed messenger from the local factory, picking up the sizable bundle of cash for the week's payroll; the young wife putting a dollar in her Christmas Club account; the local newspaper man getting his travelers checks for his trip to investigate labor conditions in the Common Market; the young couple negotiating a mortgage on the home they are buying; the farmer negotiating a loan to finance the fertilizer and seeds and labor he needs now and won't be able to pay for until the crop is harvested in the fall; the chairman of the board of the local corporation arranging the loan for a large addition to his plant; the middle-aged couple financing their new car; the clerk from the supermarket putting a few dollars into a savings account earmarked for the down payment on a house for his growing family; the teacher depositing her salary check in her checking account.

Get one of the officers of the bank to show the class what is happening right then and there in the bank. Get him to explain the functions of the bank in the field of credit and in the movement of payments and of cash. Have him tell the class what the bank does with that dollar that goes into the Christmas Club account, or with the money that supermarket clerk puts in the bank until he needs it. Have him explain how the bank can cash that social security check, where it "gets" the money to loan on that car or that factory addition. Have him tell you where the bank physically gets all the dollar bills it passes over its counters as it cashes checks, and what happens to the checks it takes in, mostly drawn on that very bank or other banks in the area but sometimes drawn on banks halfway across the continent. Ask him what the bank's relations are to the Federal Reserve system; whether deposits in the bank are insured by the Federal Deposit Insurance Corporation, and if so whether the bank pays insurance premiums as one would for one's personal insurance. Be sure to ask him what changes he has seen in banking since he joined the bank—for example, federal deposit insurance, competitive advertising for savings accounts, customer relations, and some of the many technical improvements of recent years. And when you get all through, go to the school library and read about the early banks, and wildcatting (when banks issued banknotes with little or no security to back them up or redeem them), and the National Banking Act of 1863, and the establishment of the Federal Reserve System. Then try to figure out how our economy could have gotten where it is today without banks, and what would happen if banks were abolished today.

## The Stockbroker

If there is a stockbroker in town visit his office, where you can see the ticker tape in operation and see how orders are transmitted from a distant town (yours) to the central exchange. (If this is not important to you, have him visit the classroom.) Ask him why a company issues stock—there are several reasons. Ask him how you (or he) can be assured that a given company is not a fly-by-night outfit issuing "blue sky" securities. Who buys stock, and why? How does he make his living selling other people's stocks to people in your community? How is a stock purchase registered? What kinds of stocks are there, and what are the differences? What is the risk element in a stock purchase? What is the difference between a stock and a bond? Have him review with you how your money (when you buy a stock or a bond) gets into the hands of the company that issues the stocks or bonds? What is an underwriter, and what is his function? Are all stocks and bonds listed on the major stock exchanges? If not, why not? What are the advantages of being listed, of not being listed? Here again we can get into highly sophisticated territory; or discussion can be confined to the elements which can be meaningful from the sixth grade on.

# Government

There remains the field of government. Is your community governed by a mayor and board of aldermen, or a mayor and common council, or a mayor and commission, or a commission and city manager, or some other combination? How are these officials elected or appointed? What are their legal powers? How often are elections held? Can the officials, or any one of them, be recalled? Invite one of them to meet with the class and tell you about your community government. Then visit the next meeting of the board or council and see it in action. Try to pick a meeting at which some important issue will be under discussion: the budget, a tax increase, a re-zoning proposal. Note how many citizens and representatives of citizen organizations attend. How many speak up? Did the city officials have the correct answers? To what degree did they depend on other city employees to supply the answers?

The fire department is often visited. Find out not just what happens in the event of a multiple-alarm fire, but what effect the fire department has had on property insurance rates in your community. Is it a paid department or volunteer or a combination of both? How many paid employees are there? Do firemen hold other jobs, part-time, to earn enough money to live the way they want to?

The police department is more challenging as a source of information on crime rates, crime distribution geographically and by age and social group in the community, crime detection, cooperation with county and state and federal police. They may not be interested in telling all their secrets, but a visit here, carefully pre-arranged, can be very enlightening.

So too with the welfare department, particularly if you can arrange to have the students sit with one of the interviewers for a few hours each. Here, too, a picture of the community can be found that may not otherwise be available. The class can discuss the roots and background of the problems they there encounter and so lead themselves into many segments of the community's history and society and economy. And how about the Planning Board, and the Board of Education?

Then there is the impact of the county and state and federal governments on the community. While the best place to study this is at the county seat, it may be investigated as well at the community level. Study the functions of each level of government in class, invite officials in to discuss such operations as they affect the community, then visit them in action. A day with the county agricultural agent can be very enlightening, as can one with a 4-H Club leader, the county welfare officer, the sheriff, or the county superintendent of schools.

## *The Courts*

Finally there are the courts. Not the justice of the peace or the traffic court, or even the petty larceny courts. But the civil and criminal courts, which offer opportunities to study the judicial process, the selection and function of the petit jury, the operation (which differs in different parts of the country) of the grand jury, and so forth. Invite a judge to visit the class and describe the process. Then let the class see a court in operation. Don't ask them to sit through a murder trial, or a divorce case, or an embezzlement trial, or a suit for infringement of copyright. But have them understand the process in class and how it has evolved, then give them the opportunity to see it in action.

*      *      *

Two things are clearly important. The first is that these field trips not be regarded just as junkets, as days off from the routine of the classroom. They can and should be learning experiences of major importance. They require careful preparation in advance, with the museum or with the railroad, by the teacher, in the classroom, before and after the visit. You study the history of the activity in class; you see it in operation today in the field. In the higher grades, there may have to be a follow-up visit by one or more members of the class to get information not asked for the first time but subsequently found to be needed for a full comprehension of the history and importance of the activity under study.

The second is that these field trips can be important adjuncts to the social studies at all levels. They cannot all be taken in one year or two. But one or two should be taken each semester as they fit the curriculum. It follows too that just because the railroad, for instance, was visited in kindergarten, there is no reason why it should therefore be assumed in the school that the children know all there is to know about railroading; the railroad can be visited (as can the museum, the farm, the mine, the common council) with great profit at several different grade levels through senior high school and indeed through college.

# 4

## Building
## Community
## Resources

E ACH generation of students can help the next (and, except for the first, can benefit from the work of its predecessors) in localized history by strengthening the community's collections of local materials—and incidentally learn an important fact about the development of history: that each generation builds on what has gone before. In a community of modest size, there is no point in duplicating in the school library the holdings of the public library. And in no community is it advisable to compete with an active historical society for scarce materials. But in most instances, the school should have a strong local history collection of its own, and class decisions as to what should be left to the public library and the historical society (or turned over to them if collected by the students) should be productive of useful discussion, practice in exercising judgments, and experience (for the students) in negotiating with representatives of other institutions.

## Building Library Resources

### BOOKS AND PAMPHLETS

The school library should have the books and pamphlets needed for use in the school where localized history is a live and lively subject, in addition to the copies available in the public library for adult use and reference purposes. Books and pamphlets written about the community—or the country, or region, or part of the state of which the community is a part—should be in the school library. So, too, should certain books which are peculiarly valuable for the understanding of the people or certain occupations, or institutions, or way of life in an area. These include such books (for different areas and periods) as Jared Van Wagenen, Jr., *Golden Age of Homespun* (Ithaca, N.Y., 1953); Alice M. Earle, *Stage Coach and Tavern Days* (New York, 1900); Walter P. Webb, *The Great Northwest* (New York, 1948); Thomas D. Clark, *The Southern Country Editor* (Indianapolis, 1948); Milton F. Hamilton, *The Country*

48

*Printer* (New York, 1936) ; H. E. Cole, *Stage Coach and Tavern Tales of the Old Northwest* (Cleveland, 1930) ; Robert G. Athearn, *High Country Empire* (New York, 1960) ; Paul Horgan, *Great River* (New York, 1954) ; Walter P. Webb, *The Great Plains* (Boston, 1931) ; Paul F. Sharp, *Whoop-Up Country* (Minneapolis, 1955) ; the Rivers of America and Lakes of America series; and a host of others, including the other titles in *this* series.

How acquire them? Supplement the school budget by getting parents to donate them, by raising funds to buy them, by getting a civic club, the women's club, a patriotic society, the PTA, to buy them at the request of the students.

## NEWSPAPERS

The local newspaper carries a unique record of local events and happenings. Even in the days of modern boiler plate this is true. But newspapers are delicate, particularly those printed since the advent of sulphate base papers in the 1870s. When dry and old, their pages tear easily, even crumble. They need temperature and humidity control. Is the school library the proper place for them? If not already collected in the public library, should they be given—when located—to the library? Would the library accept them? Would it bind, catalog, and care for them? Would it permit school children to use them? There are very few files of old newspapers, and frequently only one copy. They should therefore be housed in a fireproof building. Is the library fireproof? If not, is the school? Perhaps the local historical society would want them if the public library would not. Does it have a fireproof building or vault? Is its building open to the public? Is it open regularly or infrequently, or even by appointment only? Where would the newspapers have the best protection? Where would they be available to the most people? Where should they be placed, once collected?

If they have not previously been collected, where will they be found? The first place to look is the publisher's office. Most newspapers keep files of their back issues. If such a file does not exist, or has been given to the state library or the state historical society, the next best is the attics of the community. A general appeal, a little door-bell ringing, may produce wonders. Newspaper publicity on what you want and what you are doing may turn up some excellent leads. And there is always a chance that one old couple have saved the daily (or weekly) paper all their married lives and now have a file ranging back over 53 years which they will gladly present for permanent preservation to the school, or the historical society, or the library. There are opportunities here for a fine class project.

## DIARIES AND LETTERS

Diaries and letters are often very valuable sources of information on the community. What is worth saving? This can be discussed by the class at length and with value. Clearly a letter by George Washington about the surrender at

Yorktown, or about the layout of your village (now perhaps Parkersburg, W. Va.), is worth saving. In fact, because of Washington's importance, any letter written by him or even just signed by him is worth saving. But very few of these will be found in your community. What will be found are lots and lots of family diaries and letters. They present interesting problems. They are old. And because there is only one copy of the diaries and quite likely of the letters, they are unique. But are they worth saving just because they are old and unique? Or does their real value lie in what they tell us about conditions, crops, then-current events and people? The diary that simply records the time the sun rose and set and whether it was clear, cloudy, or stormy is not very significant. This information is readily available elsewhere. But the diary of the articulate farmer, businessman, lawyer, or sheriff, who records the events of the day and what he thinks of them; the letters that comment on politics, the affairs of the world, or—very importantly—the affairs of the community; these are more than worth the space they occupy. They tell us what struck at least one person at a given time and place as important enough to put in his diary or to comment on in his letters. Add a number of these together and you have something like a random sample of public opinion. And any one of them may tell us something that is nowhere else recorded about something important that was going on at that time.

If the owners are willing to part with them, and if these papers do seem worth preserving, where should they be preserved? Again the historical society and the public library are the logical alternatives to the school. Again we are dealing with unique materials of importance. Fireproof protection is very important. So is dust, heat, and temperature control. Fewer people will want to use them than will want to use the files of old newspapers, so ready access is not so important as in the case of the newspapers. Proper care, though, is just as important as for the newspapers. The correct answer as to where to place them will vary from community to community, and again will involve the students in worthwhile discussions leading to value judgments and action.

Any search of the community may turn up some very important manuscripts: perhaps a single letter from a Washington, a Jefferson, a Lincoln; perhaps the files of a former United States Senator, a Governor, a Cabinet officer, a noted author, an important inventor. This is unlikely, but possible. Such a discovery introduces a new element into the discussions of where to place the manuscripts. These are papers which scholars may want to consult with some frequency. Should they be placed in some more central repository, say the state historical society or even the Library of Congress, where they would be more readily accessible to the professional writers of American history? Or should such papers be kept in the community where they originated, or where they were found?

## ACCOUNT BOOKS AND LEDGERS

Account books and ledgers tell much of the story of the development of the community's business enterprises. So do the more complex records of the corporation. Here is basic information on price levels, wages, employment, taxes paid. But though the entries are in English and in Arabic numerals, they are hard for the novice to interpret. The books of a small business may furnish the opportunity for a short introduction to double-entry bookkeeping and a discussion of the importance of this kind of record to the businessman. The books of a large corporation may well be too complex and too voluminous for successful use below the graduate school level. This is difficult territory, but these records are a basic and provocative (and sometimes frustrating) supplement to any historical work on a particular local enterprise or industry. Again, these are unique records. For a large company they may be very bulky. More and more large companies over the last forty years have established their own archives with controls and professional staff that can be most helpful on a serious research project. While usually the company wants to keep its own old records, sometimes an efficiency expert tells the company officials that the older records are no longer worth the space they take up, and a decision is made to get rid of them. Where should they go: the historical society, the library, the school? Why?

## PHOTOGRAPHS

Photographs are one of the most fascinating types of record. Any old photograph posed in a studio will tell you something of what people wore, how they combed their hair, or in some cases how they put their heads in clamps to hold still while a time exposure was taken in the good old days. But far more revealing are the photographs of the town, the farms, the shops, the factories, the schools, the churches, street scenes, scenes of outings, excursions, games, and so forth. Here is a record of how people lived and worked and played that cannot be duplicated. These are the pictures that proverbially are worth a thousand words. Look at a shot of Main Street in 1915. What does it tell you about transportation? Are there trolley tracks? Any automobiles? Are they Stanley Steamers, or electrics, or gasoline buggies? Are there bicycles, built for one or for two? What about the condition of the pavement, the curbing, the sidewalks? What buildings are still there over a half a century later? What sort of buildings were there in 1900 or 1870? Do you notice any changes in the basic design of business buildings and stores? What can you learn from a minute inspection of this photograph about advertising techniques, store window display techniques, perhaps even prices?

Photos of the farm of earlier generations are similarly revealing of the dramatic changes from horse-and-man-power to machinery. Photos of the old-time factory may show working conditions that would not now be tolerated, lack of safety precautions, and much less complex and efficient machinery than today's. Scenes in a mine recall conditions long since abolished in all but small wildcat operations. Scenes of people going to church in their Sunday best, frolicking gingerly at the fireman's outing, digging ditches by hand for the first sewers, "bathing" in the ocean in most un-bikini-like garments, tell us much of the life of a bygone era. Cowboys on the trail or at the roundup, bronco-busters at the rodeo, farmers in the Dust Bowl, shacks of the 1920s in the Ozarks, the camps and hospitals and prisons of the Civil War (and later) capture a realism that beggars the descriptive power of the writer. A good photographic collection in the school library, therefore, is a resource for localized history that is to be treasured.

There are two major ways to build such a collection. The first is to gather existing old photos from the community; you'll find thousands. Families and relatives are a good starting point. Newspapers usually have "morgues" of old photographs, which they periodically clean out, and are glad to have the culls go to some good use. Business firms, and particularly their public relations offices, often have files of photographs of events in the history of the firm, additions to the plant, new products, and anniversary celebrations. They, too, are often willing to part with such files if they know they are going to be taken care of somewhere else in the neighborhood. Professional photographers usually keep files of the photographs they have taken, and these often include scenes of the type we have been talking about in addition to brides and chauffeurs, portraits, and family groups. But, as in the case of manuscripts, not all photos are valuable just because they are old and more or less unique. They too must tell you something to be worth saving. So be selective, careful about what you accept for your collections.

If old photographs are collected, the collector should get all possible information from the donor: the identity of the scene and of the people in the picture, the approximate date of the photo, and the name of the donor. These should be lightly pencilled on the back of the photo as a minimum; better still, the photo can be mounted and the data entered on the bottom or back of the mount; best of all, each photo may be inserted in an envelope of appropriate size, and each envelope labelled with this information. But many photos, many people in certain photos (such as the grammar school graduating class of 1905) will remain unidentified. So stage a Photo Identification Night. Invite parents, old folks, members of the local historical society, anyone interested, to help with what has not yet been properly identified. They will have a lot of fun, and you will get a lot of information—and probably the offer of more photographs from some of those present.

But you should also start your own up-to-date collection for the use of future students. If the school has a camera club, get its members interested and enlist their help. Or start a camera section of your history club, or use the camera hounds in the class. Set up a continuing project. This year photograph everything about one topic: say Industry. Explain your project to the owner or manager of the plant and get his cooperation. Get outside views, inside views, products, key staff, shipping procedures, everything you can. Be sure each photo is accurately identified, labelled, and dated. Next year do Farming (or Dairying or Ranching or whatever is appropriate in your community). Next year take Transportation, and photograph everything from the old trolley car converted into a diner to the interstate highway and the dirt road over the hill to X's farm; shots of the newest and oldest trucks and autos and busses on the road; the railroad right-of-way, station, equipment, signals, etc.; the airport, some of the different types of planes using its facilities, its control tower, its repair hangars; the river and riverboats (if any) or the lake transportation (if any), the port, the loading and unloading and storage facilities. Then year by year take other topics: education, religion, recreation, government, communication. When all the topics have been covered once, your successors should begin all over again: industry, farming, transportation, etc. Think what a treasure trove later classes will enjoy. Think what you would have at your disposal if such a program had been instituted twenty or fifty or a hundred years ago in your community. And be sure that this is set up as part of the annual program of the grade or club, because the value of such a project increases in geometric progression each year that it is carried on.

Outside this regular, organized, annual program, be alert for special occasions when photographs would be useful for the historical file. When a state highway is about to be relocated near town, photograph the existing right of way, the survey parties, the grading operations, the new pavement. When an old building is about to be demolished—the opera house, an early residence, the court house, the antiquated gasoline station—photograph its exterior, its interior, the process of demolition, the hole in the ground, the new foundations, the new structure. When the President of the United States, or the Apostolic Delegate, or a United States Senator, or an astronaut, comes to town, record the event. When plans are announced for a new subdivision on the farm outside of town (or the golf course is sold for the same purpose), photograph the farm—house, barns, fields (or the golf course)—then the bulldozers at work, the first houses, the laying of water pipes, sewer pipes, electric and telephone cables, curbs, and the street paving. When plans are announced for the new dam which will augment the community's water supply or add handsomely to the available electrical power, photograph the site, the brook or river, the valley and its farms, then the work of construction and finally the dam in full operation and the lake in the valley behind it. Or when the railroad spur through town is abandoned, photograph the last train, then the equipment ripping up the rails, and finally the abandoned right-of-way. This is the sort of historical record your successors, and your children and your children's children, will cherish and bless you for having established.

Because anyone can start a project like this, and the local historical society should be doing so on its own, the problem of where to keep the files is not as important here as in the case of newspapers and manuscripts. But the local historical society or the public library might want such a file, and over the years it might be better cared for and seen and used by more people if kept in one of these other places. Here again is a chance for discussion and value judgment. Just be sure that if the decision is to keep the file in the school library, provision is made for its use by adults who may be interested.

## FILMS

Still cameras are not the only kind that the students are apt to have available. There may also be at least one movie camera in the class (at the secondary school level). And moving pictures can be even more useful than stills in recording historical events of certain types. Some local events are worth filming. For instance, the folk dances in the nearby Polish (or Swedish or any other nationality) neighborhood. Film them and preserve them. But also study them, practice them, dance them. Film the last passenger train to operate on the local branch line (and tape the sounds), and preserve it. Or the dedication of the new power station, the opening of the new post office, the erection of the new television station broadcasting tower, the opening of the new bridge. Or the final encampment of the Spanish-American War veterans of the area. Or the local historical house as it was when the decision was made to preserve it; the various stages of restoration; the dedication. Or before and after automation shots of work in the local factory or refinery or post office or market. These films may be of little immediate significance to the class, but in a very few years they will be treasured—and not just by the students of the next generation. Here is another activity where the students can help build for others, for the future.

Films, like manuscripts, require special housing—specifically, constant temperature and humidity. Where should they be preserved: school, or library, or historical society? And why?

## TAPE RECORDINGS

Another important historical resource is the tape recording. The perfection of inexpensive, efficient, and nearly foolproof recorders has added a major new dimension to the gathering and preservation of historical source material. There are at least three major fields in which the recorder can be used to great advantage—all, obviously, in the field of preserving sounds.

What sorts of sounds are worth preserving? First the oral reminiscences of a person who has lived some significant segments of the community's life.

This means an interview, or a series of interviews. The interview is a tricky thing, to be conducted with skill and care. It is hardly conceivable in the elementary grades, but satisfactory jobs can be undertaken in senior high school. As indicated earlier (p. 32), the person conducting the interview should know as much as possible about the field to be covered before it starts. He needs this information to be able to keep the person interviewed on the track, to prevent him or her from wandering off the subject or from ducking the point of the interview (such as why the mayor really vetoed that ordinance to permit the erection of a slaughterhouse next to the city park, or why the district leader really switched his support from one candidate to another in the 1946 election). He needs the full consent and cooperation of the person to be interviewed. He must be sure that the interviewee is not "afraid" of the recorder and will not freeze when he sees a microphone in front of him. Then he has to have (or develop) a skilled ear for how much "rambling" to permit. The tangents an interviewee takes are sometimes most productive; generally they are a great waste of time. The tape can be edited and erased, but the time is gone forever.

Why such recordings? A good deal of local history dies each time a leader in politics, business, or the professions dies. Few people these days keep diaries. Few busy men or women have the time to write their memoirs. But they will take a few hours to sit down with another person and answer questions and recall what they can for the recorder. Much can then be captured that otherwise would be lost forever. The recorder, too, can do much to supplement the files of the articulate letter writer and the newspaper accounts of events with behind-the-scenes information, with inside stuff, particularly with the motivation behind men's acts—*why* who did what he did.

There are other sounds worth preserving. One thinks of the folk songs of the area, both those that some of the oldest men and women may remember from their childhood in the neighborhood and those brought in by people from other areas and from other nations across the seas. These are part of the cultural heritage of the community, and despite all the recording that has been done and all the revived interest of the present generation in folksongs, many are still unrecorded. In any case, the experience of recording these songs is worthwhile; the act of doing it oneself adds a special, indelible educational fillip. The music may not be of La Scala quality. The singer's explanation of the history and significance of the song may not be entirely authentic. But both are part of the local cultural scene and worth preserving.

Comparative studies with comparable songs (and explanations) are possible for the class in the many recordings sponsored by the Library of Congress, the several folklore societies, many historical societies. The standard bibliography is Charles Haywood's *A Bibliography of North American Folklore and Folksong* (New York, 1961).

There is a third category of sounds worth preserving: those that are quite typical of today but are about to pass from the scene. The voices of prominent local leaders in business and the professions, labor and the arts, as well as in politics, will one day have historical interest. We know precisely what Theodore Roosevelt and Enrico Caruso sounded like because we have recordings of their voices. We have only written descriptions of Lincoln's voice, not even that about Ralph Waldo Emerson. Recordings of the voices of local leaders—the state senator, the local assemblymen, the mayor, the superintendent of schools, the local newspaper editor, for instance—outlining the major problems of the community today and suggesting their solutions would in ten or a hundred years be a fascinating file for the students then in the school, and for a lot of other people as well.

The sound of the whistle of the steam locomotive, once a familiar call all across the country, is all but gone. The riveter's drill is almost silenced. The sound of the lake steamer, the river tug, the old-style siren of the fire engine, the coyote, the wagon, the hand-operated forge, wheels on a cobblestone pavement: these and a thousand other sounds are becoming less and less familiar. And many sounds common enough today will follow them into first rarity and then oblivion. Preservation of such sounds is perhaps the least important of the uses of the recorder which we have considered. Yet these sounds are part of the surroundings in which our community has lived, part of the aura of the past. And they might one day prove as helpful to the sound effects people in dramatics groups as to the historians.

Tapes, like manuscripts, require special care. They must be housed under proper conditions of heat and humidity. Again there are questions of where they should be preserved—school, historical society, library—and why.

A well-planned, continuing program of collecting printed materials (books, pamphlets, newspapers, programs, and throw-aways), manuscript materials (letters, diaries, and business records), photographs, movies, and tape recordings of historical value to the community can be a significant experience and can add greatly to the resources of the community for its own history. It can make the students intimately aware of heritage, can involve them in an ongoing program, can yield tangible results of permanent value to the community.

## Building Museum Resources

The museum has long been recognized as an instrument of general public education second in importance only to the public library. To actually see and perhaps handle the objects of the past brings the practices of that past to life with a reality that lies beyond the reach of the written or printed word. Displays of objects therefore have an important function to perform in the school that is concerned with community history.

Many schools have such displays in their corridors, along the walls of the library or the cafeteria, in some instances in a special room (perhaps in the base-ment). The special room is ideal, but space is at a premium in most school buildings today and corridor and wall facilities are all that can be expected.

Displays can be housed in cases (wall cases or table cases), or panels (large for wall or free-standing display; small to rest on the blackboard chalk-trays), or on tables. They can include photographs, sketches, maps, charts, models, and dioramas, as well as replicas and objects. There must be identifying and descrip-tive labels to help the objects tell a tight, cohesive story. If space simply cannot be found within the school building, an enterprising group will easily secure the use of some vacant store windows downtown, or the abandoned depot, or some suitable spot for the cases and the display.

Here is another activity in which many interests and talents, and conceivably several parts of the school curriculum, can be combined in a school project. Some students can locate and bring in materials for the displays. Others can record or "accession" them, or make out records so that objects loaned for a particular exhibit can be returned promptly when the exhibit is over. Some, perhaps in art class, can make sketches, models, dioramas, or special background mounts for displays. Others, perhaps in industrial arts class, can make display cases.

Let's begin with the objects for display. Our displays are going to be con-fined to community history. What sort of objects do we want?

First of all, things germane to the community. Things that tell us about the people to whom they belonged: where the owners came from, what they did for a living, how they lived, what they ate and how they cooked it, how they dressed, how they were cared for when they were ill, what they did with their spare time, if any. What sort of objects tell us things like that? Objects brought from the former home back East (or North or South or West); objects valuable enough to bring along from the Old Country. It tells us something about our forebears that grandma treasured the copper kettle, three bonehandled forks, a coverlet, and an icon enough to bring them in the steerage to the new country. Then there are the tools with which great-grandfather and his father made their living: farm tools perhaps, crude by comparison with what is available today; perhaps even an iron-sheathed wooden plow, an old A-drag, a simple wooden hand-operated seeder; or the leaching stone and barrel for securing the lye with which to make soap, the huge iron kettle for boiling syrup, or an elaborate sling in which to immobilize obstreperous oxen while shoeing them. There are the articles from the old kitchen with its cistern pump and wood burning stove: the cast-iron baking tins, the apple parer, the coffee grinder, the spice tins. There are tools from the shop: the tools of the cooper, the carpenter, the cobbler, the tinsmith, the tanner, or the blacksmith. Perhaps there is an adze, a blade from an up-and-down saw pit, a miner's lamp. There are things from the home: a flax-brake, hetchels, spinning wheel, loom; candle dip or candle mold; perhaps a bed-warmer, with the vision it conjures up of ice-cold beds far from the hearth;

or the thundermug which spared one a midnight trip through three feet of snow to the privy. Perhaps it is a handmade chair (if you're lucky, a chair hewn from the trunk of a large basswood tree), or a colorful hand-sewn coverlet, or a hooked rug. Perhaps it is a model of the device grandpa patented. Perhaps it is a model of the *Clermont* that father took in at the store in settlement of a bad debt. Perhaps it is a Mason jar, which every frugal housewife not too many years ago used to can the surplus goods from the family garden. It really is not important to know a froe from a whiffle-tree; the important thing is for the student to see how much hard work went into simple operations in the days before machines, what our forefathers really had to do to earn a living and how relatively little they could produce in a given hour of labor compared with what can be done today.

Whatever it is, it has a story to tell, a story bearing on the history of the community and on the people who lived there and left it as their monument. Such objects can be put together in meaningful exhibits on the way people lived, or the way they dressed, or how they made dyes, or how they cured tobacco, or how and why they built the covered bridge that used to span the creek, or how they built the local canal, or how they enjoyed themselves at the shooting match, or with skittles or hand-wrought horseshoes, or bowling on the green, or square dancing, or barn-raising.

Objects tell these stories. So do photographs, models, and dioramas. It is hard to bring an old-time farm, a railroad locomotive, or an early iron furnace into the classroom or the school. But in miniature, as a model or as a diorama, it is simple, and the model is both visible and easy to understand.

The objects are to be found in the community: in attics, in barns, or nearby farms, in cellars, in unexpected caches in warehouses. Modern suburbs and big cities are apt to be short of farm implements and blacksmith tools, but if you can't find what you want and need, try the local historical society. See if they have and will lend you for a special exhibit what you can't find yourself. And if they don't have it, or are already using it in an exhibit of their own, try the state museum, or the museum in the large city nearby. Objects on loan must be treated with great care and returned to the donor promptly and in exactly as good condition as they were in when they arrived.

Sketches, models and dioramas, the backgrounds and mounts, the show cases should be made in the school. Simple, inexpensive, and very useful show cases can readily be constructed. Simple dioramas and models are not too difficult to make. Remember that the displays must be organized to tell a story, and explanatory labels, maps, diagrams, and sketches should supplement the objects and photographs and models to make that story clear.

These exhibits can be semi-permanent, held over from year to year, added to year by year, the additions being coordinated with special research projects in community history for that year. When the class is working on the story of transportation, you should get your transportation photographs, models, and time-tables, an Indian traverse, a dug-out canoe; when the class is working on the story of the farm, get objects typical of the old-time farm home; when the class is working on the history of education in the community, dig out old photographs of earlier school buildings, athletic and social events, old textbooks, old class grade books, and the several types of desks, benches, and stools, slates, globes, and other paraphernalia of the classroom. Add one or two such exhibits each year, and before long the school will have a museum which will be a teaching resource of genuine significance and a memorable exercise for the students who partici-pate. It will also deservedly attract the attention of the entire community.

Or the exhibits can be temporary, done each year, geared to the course in American history: Indian period (local), early settlement (local), agriculture (local), education (local), etc. If a picture is "worth a thousand words," so too is seeing and handling a tomahawk or dream drum, a primitive cultivator, a tanner's knife, a churn, a grapevine cradle, a blacksmith's bellows, a schnitzel-bank.

At all times, keep in touch with the local historical society and, if it is separate, the local museum. If they do not exist in your community, there will be one of each nearby. They, the state historical society, and the state museum will be most helpful with ideas, with technical advice, and perhaps with the loan of objects the students cannot find elsewhere in the vicinity. They will help locate items, identify them, give advice on how to care for them. The American Association for State and Local History has issued a series of "Technical Leaflets" which will tell you in reasonably simple terms how to care for that leather harness or that iron tool.[1] And perhaps you can help the local historical society by turning over to them an item you may come across which they need.

---

[1] Write the Association at 132 Ninth Avenue North, Nashville, Tennessee 37203, for information.

# 5

## Special
## Activities

THE program of understanding America by studying the community, gathering materials for library and museum, doing research and writing, visiting businesses, industries, transportation centers, and government, can be supplemented by other activities, many of them right inside the same school. The class involved in community history quickly discovers that it can use all sorts of help. As it becomes more deeply involved in the field, its enthusiasm grows; and greater enthusiasm seems to encourage more assistance from others. Groups other than the social studies classes can readily be involved, to the educational benefit of all concerned.

## Involving the Rest of the School

### DRAMATICS

The dramatics group, whether class or club, is one of the first to call to your side. There are three ways it can be involved. The first is the historical play. This can be based on an episode or episodes or a period or a movement in the history of the community. It can be built around one person—the man who founded the town, or some famous figure in politics or business or the arts who lived there. It can be built around a group of people. The script for the play may already exist, or the students working on community history may sit down with the students in the theater program or in English classes to work out the elements of the play and perhaps help write it. Or the teacher (or teachers) may want to do the script, with student cooperation and consultation. Or there may be a playwright in town who will volunteer for the assignment.

A second way—often more successful—to enlist the drama group is the historical pageant. Here is presented episode by episode the history of the town: the Indian days, the Revolution (if the community is that old—or the Texas Revolution, or the Bear Flag Republic, or whatever), the first settlement, the first mills, water transportation (perhaps the opening of a canal), the coming of the railroad, the Civil War, etc., down to the present. Or the pageant may present the story of a period in the town's history: during the Sioux Uprising, the dream dances, the Fenian invasion, or the Lincoln-Douglas debates.

Perhaps the town was once a station on the Underground Railroad, or was the site of a major riot (a 19th-century labor disturbance, a race riot, or a Civil War draft protest). Perhaps it produced a famous statesman, a writer, or an astronaut. Around any of these or a myriad of other topics the episodes of a good historical pageant can be constructed. The students who have done the research can spot or help spot the significant themes or events around which to construct the various scenes.

The play is confined to a relatively small stage; the pageant can roam widely. The play may need elaborate scenery and backdrops; the pageant usually has none. At a play, the audience must be within sound of the actor's voice; in a pageant only the narrator, aided by a public address system, need be heard. In a play all the actors must memorize lines; in a pageant all they need to do is to move through their roles in measured pantomime while the narrator tells the story. The pageant, a somewhat lower art form than the play, is therefore both more flexible and easier to rehearse and stage. (It is also, if held outdoors, sub ject to the weather.)

The third area for participation of those interested in drama appears whenever the school is given time for a radio or television play. Radio is much the simpler and much more likely. It requires only a good script, tailored to fit radio time schedules, and good student voices or oral actors to read it. Rehearsals can be held in the schoolroom. Television is a very different medium, having all the requirements of a play before an audience and some very special differences. Lines must be learned, acting is physical as well as oral, actors must get used to cameras intruding on the stage, voices must reach not the back of the auditorium but merely the nearby microphone. The major problem, which makes school plays on TV so very rare, is that the camera crews must also be rehearsed. This means that rehearsals take place at the studio rather than in the classroom; and this in turn involves tying up expensive studio time and equipment for many long rehearsals and frequent script revisions. It is therefore unlikely that even for community history plays your group will get TV time from the local station. It is possible, but radio time is much more likely. But in either type of presentation, your colleagues and associates in drama can be very helpful. The participating students have the satisfaction not only of mastering new skills and techniques but of sharing their new knowledge of community history with a wider audience.

## INDUSTRIAL ARTS

The industrial arts department, as already suggested, can be of very basic help in the display program. Here can be built table cases, wall cases, easels, and special mounts that a good exhibit demands. Simple machines to operate exhibit turntables or automated exhibits can be made. Sound effects, tripped by push-button or by photoelectric cell, can be wired into the exhibits. So can automated slide projections and taped descriptions of parts of the exhibit (or the story or purpose of the exhibit, or of the program in community history). So can illuminated maps which show a particular site when the identifying button is pressed, or quiz boards which buzz or fire off Roman candles when you connect the right answer to the right question. All these props can be prepared in industrial arts, where the students again master new techniques and have the real satisfaction of doing so in the interests of a larger project on which many of their contemporaries are also working in other ways.

## THE ART DEPARTMENT

The art department can also be very helpful. Here both two- and three-dimensional exhibit materials can be prepared for cases in corridors, library, cafeteria, or museum room. Sketches or water colors caricaturing a certain action essential to the story of a display (Mr. Lincoln speaking at Gettysburg, the first stage coach into town, the wreck of a whaler on the coast) can be prepared at any grade level. Charts and graphs are vital to many exhibits. So are maps. And finally there are dioramas, which can range from utmost simplicity to highly technical resolutions of perspectives and the difficult blending of proscenium into the foreground. And if the products of the students' efforts are to be used in some public display, as in the corridors or a History Fair (see below), they again have obvious utility and will receive merited recognition from the rest of the student body and the visiting public.

## HOME ECONOMICS

The home economics department can share the fun. Some of the problems of pioneer living take on a new reality for the girl who tries baking over an open fire, or churning her own butter and smoothing it free of watery residue on a butter table, or dipping her own candles, or leaching wood ash to get the lye from which to make soap. Or curing raw flax (perhaps grown right on the school grounds), braking and hetchelling it, spinning it into linen thread of uneven consistency, and then feeding the thread into an old-fashioned loom and weaving it into cloth. (If the school does not have a hand loom, the local museum probably does.) Or making that cloth—or even store cloth—into clothes, particularly the many-layered canopies which swathed the female figure until after World War I. (These clothes could be made for a historical fashion show, or for costumes for the play or pageant or TV show.) Preparing various colonial and pioneer recipes can be fun, and preliminary to a special school feast, perhaps at Thanksgiving time. Cooking and preparing the food specialties of various nationality groups can be instructive, too. Everyone in town, even the descendants of the Indians, is descended from immigrants, so almost everyone should have some European or Asiatic or African recipes to contribute. English scones or crumpets, Scandinavian lefse and krummkake or a good smorgasbord, Italian lasagna, Jewish blintzes and bagels, Greek honey pie or meats baked in grape leaves, yogurt, Rumanian alivenci or tocana, Turkish (and other) pilafs, Peking duck and Chinese chicken velvet, the special delights from France—bouillabaisse, poisson en patisserie, filet mignon—and a thousand and one other recipes from abroad can be put to use in the ovens, stoves, and kettles of home economics. And they can be a novel and delightful feature of a Folk Fair or History Fair. With the recipes go hand in hand the story of the people who brought them to the community.

## MUSIC

The music department will be interested in folk songs of the area: the songs the first settlers brought with them, folk songs from various other countries, the local variants or new verses local troubadours put to old folk tunes. And the language arts people can be enlisted here. As foreign languages enter the curriculum of more and more grade schools, and more and more languages are taught in the secondary schools, the songs of the French-Canadian voyageur, the Italian vineyard worker, or the itinerant wetback of the southwest are no longer beyond the reach of the student. They give new dimensions both to the history of the community and to the music program. They offer ready-made opportunities to share knowledge with others in programs for assemblies, for PTA meetings, for luncheon, service, and women's clubs, and for radio and local TV, which will enrich the local American culture and open additional insights into the history and heritage of the community. And with the songs go always the stories of the people who first sang them in your neighborhood.

## PHYSICAL EDUCATION

The physical education department in many schools already does something with folk dancing. Here again, in addition to the typical American barn dances, the folk dances of the other nationality groups represented in the community are just as good exercise, physically and aesthetically: Polish, Dutch, Ukrainian, Greek, Swedish, Norwegian, Irish, and so on. There will be somebody in town who knows some of these dances and can teach them to the students or to the physical education staff. And again a new dimension will be added to the understanding of the history of the community and a new fillip to the physical education program and the local culture.

# The History Fair

All these activities supplement and round out the study of the community story in social studies. They can be brought together in an increasingly common phenomenon: the History Fair. The great success of the Science Fair in the secondary schools in recent years is now paralleled in many schools by that of the History Fair. This, too, is an annual event, in which the students share with the community, their parents, and their fellow students what they have been learning and doing in community history: in special programs; in research and writing and publishing localized history; in collecting materials for the school library (or the historical society or public library) and for the display areas in the school; in making dioramas and models and display backgrounds; in collecting, identifying, and taking photographs showing the development of the community and various aspects of its life and activities. The folk dances learned in physical education and folk songs learned in music can be a spectacular part of the program. Plays, pageants, skits can be represented by short selections, photographs, or movies—or the fair may go on for several evenings so that all activities can be seen in full. The costumes made in home economics can be worn, and the cooking sampled at refreshment time. These fairs are a fine occasion for summarizing and bringing together the year's work and for sharing new knowledge and new achievements with a wider audience. They also frequently supply eye-popping reminders to the parents of what their children can do when challenged. The community, too, will be pleasantly surprised at the extent, variety, and imagination of your displays.

## Folk Fairs

Comparable to the History Fair is the Folk Fair. This is more specialized, and it too is a valuable educational venture which is always popular with the community.

The purpose of the Folk Fair is to acquaint the people of the community (and the rest of the student body) with the customs, foods, products, and costumes of various nationality groups whose descendants are represented in the community, and thus to lead to further understanding of the community's heritage. You can get all kinds of help from the ethnic groups themselves. The range of program possibilities is enormous and easily sufficient to enlist the resources of many departments in the school.

Nationality dishes (which can be sold to an inquisitive and appreciative public) can be prepared in home economics. So, too, can the native costumes for both boys and girls. Folk dancing can be practiced under the physical education staff; singing under the music department. There can be exhibits of the contributions of the citizens of Irish or Polish or Syrian descent to the economy and society of the community. There can be pictures and biographical sketches of prominent citizens of German or Hungarian or Chinese ancestry. There can be a healthy emphasis on "travel in your own community"—you really don't have to go abroad for a rich experience. And from the whole fair comes a new community awareness and enjoyment of its varied cultural background. As Russell H. Conwell used to preach, there are acres of diamonds right in your own backyard.

## Historical Markers

Have all the important historic sites in your community been marked? Almost certainly not. Here is another significant adjunct to the student's work in community history. As they study, as they conduct their research, they are going to find out that a particular location—not just the town, but the northeast corner of Main and Third streets—is where something really significant happened. This particular spot is where uranium was first discovered in the area. This is where the old ferry crossed the river. This is where the westward trail to Santa Fé went through town. Here one of the great cattle trails—the Chisholm, the Humboldt, the Shawnee—crossed the river, and here is the site of the Wells Fargo or the Pony Express station. This is where the old academy stood; this is where the abolitionist press was wrecked. Here a major skirmish of a local Indian war took place; here a noted suffragette was born. This is where the old quarry which supplied all the stone for the buildings in the center of town was located. This is where a major political reform convention was held. This is where the old fort stood. Here the army camped en route to Armageddon. This is the oldest building in town. Sites of political, economic, military, social, and cultural significance are all grist for the mill, all possible places to commemorate with markers.

There will be problems involved. Like so much old-style local history, you will find much myth, much romanticized folklore about where things happened and what happened there. Make sure of the facts through careful research before you set about erecting a marker. You will have to decide what you are going to consider a historic site: the birthplace of a national figure who moved away at the age of two? the house to which a famous man retired at 76, to die a year later? a notable piece of American Gothic gingerbread? the right-of-way of the railroad that never was built? the site of the Indian garbage pit? Such sites clearly are not so important as some of those mentioned in the preceding paragraph. And not all of the preceding group are of equal significance. So you will have to establish priorities, if you are to mark the more important sites first. Here careful research, consultation with the local historical society and others knowledgable in community history, and your own best judgment are required.

How mark a site? The simplest and least expensive way is to put a small wooden sign with a number on it at the curb or on the front wall of the building. Or the number can be painted (with the permission of the city fathers) on the pavement of the street—not in the parking strip where it will be covered by parked cars. Property owners usually offer the least objections to this, the poorest form of marking. Then a printed or mimeographed folder can be prepared giving a brief sketch of each by its identifying number. Include a caution that this site is privately owned and visitors are not welcome, or the owner will be pestered by visitors and may demand that the marker be removed. A better way is to erect a wooden marker with a very brief description of the significance of the site printed right on it. Such wooden markers can be prepared in industrial arts class.

But paint fades and wood rots. Metallic markers (cast iron or aluminum) are far more durable; their finishes—baked on—need renewal only once in a decade. It may be possible to have these made at very low cost in the vocational or technical school, or in the state prison. If they have to be obtained commercially (and there are a number of firms specializing in such markers) they will cost at least $150, depending on the size, style, number of words in the label, etc. But high school students know how to raise money in many, many ways. And they are effective solicitors with the Chamber of Commerce, individual industries, the patriotic societies, and others who might finance a permanent marker.

Markers should be legible. Neither the pedestrian nor the passenger in the automobile is usually equipped with field glasses or a maginfying glass. He should not need to use either in order to read the marker. Markers should be placed where they can be seen. The front of a building, not the back; on the highway rather than in the middle of the woods; outside the cave rather than in it, is the place for the marker. And the markers should be designed so as not to create traffic hazards—outside of town on state or county highways a drive-out should be planned so that cars can pull off the fast-moving traffic lanes to stop for a look; inside town they should be readable at a glance or parking facilities should be provided nearby. Permission to erect such markers must be secured: from the property owner and from the town council. Securnig such permission is not only necessary but also is another good experience for the student.

Once the markers are in place, whether full-scale metallic markers or wooden ones or numbers painted on the pavement, the group can work out a tour of the sites, so that the visitor can move from one site to another in their chronological order and so get a bird's-eye view of the story of the town; or from one site to the next nearest geographically, which the traffic department will favor. This calls for a map in a descriptive brochure of the sites. Perhaps the city fathers will permit the school to supplement this map by painting arrows of a distinctive color—green, or pink, or something not ordinarily used for traffic or parking directions—at intersections to indicate the turns a driver following this tour should make to reach the next site. Such pavement markings are most helpful, saving a lot of neck craning to pick up street signs and a good many missed turns.

Special values here? The effective presentation of materials to teach the citizen and the tourist something of community history. The experience of negotiating with property owners and city officials to secure the necessary permissions, and with vocational schools or prison officials or commercial producers to procure the markers. And perhaps the public recognition that will come to the group for a program well conceived and well executed—or the troubles that will accompany the opposite sort of performance.

## *Inventory of Historical Objects*

A highly intriguing project which can be undertaken in any school district is an inventory of historical objects in private hands. This is a broadside extension of the selective collecting of library and museum materials suggested earlier in this chapter to build up historical resources of the community. This project is different in that (1) it is an inventory, not an acquisition program; (2) it is all-inclusive, not confined to materials for the library or the display; (3) even though directed to listing only materials of significance just to the history of *your* community, it is almost certain to uncover some items of broader interest.

First your group must decide what you are going to consider historical objects for the purposes of this survey. The types of things discussed earlier represent a good starting point: books, articles, pamphlets, and reprints on the history of the community, the county, and the state, or on selected topics germane to the history of the community (the stagecoach tavern, the country doctor, the small-town editor, the rural church, etc.) ; unpublished manuscripts on the same subjects; files of local newspapers; printed reports and documents; manuscript letters, diaries, account books; the articles people brought with them from earlier homes in the States or abroad; the tools they used; the clothes they wore; the kitchen implements; the furniture, furnishings, and equipment of the home, shop, mill, or mine.

Then prepare a form. It should show the name of the person you interview, his address, the historical objects he or she has. On an interview, you should explain carefully what *you* consider historical, for not everyone will think of the old iron skillet in the kitchen, or the tin lantern hanging on a rafter in the garage. And not everyone will realize that great-grandfather's diary of pioneering in Iowa is historical. So explain your mission carefully. Advance publicity for the project in the local newspaper and over the local radio station will help. So will appeals for cooperation through the local service clubs, the women's clubs, church groups, and other organizations. Let the community know that the survey is coming. It should be understood that you are not trying to take anything away from anybody, that you just want to know where things are and someday might ask to borrow a particular item for a particular exhibit. Then go to work. Have your form mimeographed. Be sure one is filled out for each call each student makes, even if there is nothing to report except the fact that the call was made, and that the report indicates whether the reception was friendly or hostile. Divide your district into blocks or other segments, assign one to each student with instructions to call at every home and every apartment and every store in his assigned area.

The results will be amazing. Historic items have a way of moving around the country far from their places of origin. Someone in the family treasures an object and takes it with him when he moves from Maine to California. But when he dies in California, no one else in the family shares his enthusiasm, and the object is sold to a junkman, who sells it to another person who later moves to Florida. A colleague of mine found in Racine, Wisconsin, the minute book of an association of the British physicians and surgeons attached to the British army of occupation of New York City during the Revolutionary War. I found the papers of a United States senator from Wisconsin on an estate in Maryland, and those of a congressman in the basement of a New York City apartment. Your community, no matter how large or how small, will have an extraordinary range of historical materials, and this inventory will be a way of uncovering their existence. Knowing where things are will be very useful when you need a certain object for an exhibit; it will be equally useful to the local historical society. And you may find something in Ohio that clearly belongs in the Nebraska State Historical Society (which would love to hear about your discovery), or something in New York that clearly belongs in Utah. Here is a new opportunity for a new type of pen-pal operation, as well as adding to the corpus of community knowledge, gaining valuable experience in calling on strangers, and helping the local historical society as well as others that are far afield.

## Heirloom Shows

Sometime have every member of the class bring in a family heirloom: something from the farm, something from the old country, something from the war; a letter, a tool, a kitchen implement, an antimacassar, a candle-mold, a pair of old spectacles—anything that has a story behind it. Have each student identify the object, tell— if this is not obvious—what it was used for and how, and then give the story of the role it played in his family's history. This can make an interesting special program, which may be worth repeating before the school assembly and even worth inviting parents and other adults to see and to participate in.

## Family History

Family history, like local history, has acquired something of a bad name in many quarters, due entirely to the abuse of a fundamentally respectable field. Like the old-style local history, family history is frequently befogged with myths and fairy tales, unsupported by any existing evidence or any faint likelihood of reality. In many instances it is a not altogether admirable form of ancestor worship.

But if localized, or community, history is of great educational importance to the student because of the propinquity and familiarity of materials, how much more so the history of his own family. Later in life he will probably come to see how much he is the creature of his forebears, how much he owes them not only in physical inheritance but in intellectual outlook and cultural sensitivity. This is not to deprecate the importance of environment; it is merely to suggest that one's inheritance is important, it is interesting, it is encouraging in that it often appears to have so little connection with the social status of the family.

Family history can range from the simplest genealogical charts on which, in the early grades, the student fills in the names of his parents and of their parents (this is as far as many will be able to go) and their occupations. It can move in later grades to the preparation of short biographical sketches of parents and grandparents, with a healthy respect for the black sheep as well as the luminaries. In many cases the family chart can be carried back additional generations. It is a good experience for the student to find that one grandfather set type on a small-town newspaper, while another worked on the New York piers. It does no harm to find out that one's forebears were just plain, ordinary, hard-working folk, with an occasional bum in the lot. It can have a healthy, leavening influence wherever a child has a tendency to snobbishness; it can have an equally healthy effect in inculcating a sense of respect for the hard work that ancestors put into a life no self-respecting child today would tolerate as a prospective career for himself.

This exercise will be more successful in middle-class communities than among the culturally deprived, where family records are so frequently incomplete and, where known, not always enlightening. You may want to ascertain beforehand the degree to which any culturally deprived children in your group can participate before initiating this type of project. Some, where only poverty is the problem, will be able to contribute royally; others would be seriously handicapped.

## *"Century" Farms and Families*

In urban and rural communities alike, the family that has resided in the same house or on the same farm for a hundred years or more holds special interest. The city house, like the farmhouse and the barns, is apt to contain accumulated items that other families would have thrown out when they moved, and so be a storehouse of things you might want for your school exhibits, or that would interest the local historical society, or that would necessitate several calls when inventorying the historical treasures of the community. Such "century residences" may also furnish some surprises. There is a tendency in some quarters to regard the first settlers, the "old families," with a certain artificial veneration —sometimes deserved, sometimes not. The family may have been very successful in many ways, may have found in the community all the challenge and all the satisfaction it needed. But on the other hand the failure to move west, the farming of the same soil generation after generation, may indicate instead a lack of imagination or courage, a willingness to "stay sot" which may not have produced the highest type of intellect or the most successful citizen. Whatever the personal reasons, whatever the motivations of a hundred years, properties that have been in the hands of one family for a full century are always full of interesting things. And the people who have stayed in one community despite the extraordinary mobility of our normal or average population are apt to be interesting too.

## *Programs for Adult Audiences*

In addition to a History Fair, plays and pageants, possible radio and unlikely television plays, there are many other program opportunities outside the classroom through which a group working on community history can share its hard-won knowledge.

Just as America for over a century and a quarter has been generally convinced of the importance of education, so students performing have an ineffable, apparently irresistible, appeal. From the finger painting of the kindergarten and the strident discords of a fifth grade "symphony" to the polished efforts of the chorus of the senior high school, the adult is enraptured. He loves it all.

No group is more easily captivated by the younger generation's efforts in community history than the adults interested in the same field. An annual appearance before the local historical society, featuring formal "papers" or reports, skits, panel discussions, quiz games, or even "spell-downs" using facts of community history with a panel of historical society members, is guaranteed to have the adults on the edge of their chairs for the evening and to give the younger generation an interesting experience, too.

Similarly, the service and women's clubs are always on the lookout for programs that offer something new and different to their sometimes jaded members. No luncheon club, no patriotic society, no women's club will be bored at the end of any program on the history of the community put on by their juniors. And so for veterans organizations, church groups, PTA meetings. At any gathering of parents or citizens, programs of all and any sorts by the school children are more than welcome, while the experience of performing before adults and strangers is excellent training for children who will be doing just that the rest of their lives in one way or another.

## Radio or Television

This same appeal of youth and youthful effort carries over the air. Just as adults like to hear and see young students perform in person, they welcome them on the radio. Managers of local radio stations know this. They also are on the lookout for programs of local interest. The combination of youth and community history is made to order for them. So when your group has some good reports stemming from its research, let the manager of the local station know. Chances are excellent that he will find program time for it. He is apt to be even more receptive to an interview of some of the young researchers, or the inventoriers of local historical treasures, where a station emcee can ask the students about what they are doing. Such programs have a spontaneity that adds much to their appeal. Panel discussions by the young historians, either among themselves or with adult participants, and quiz shows, either all young or again of mixed ages, are also excellent air copy.

Having indicated that young people's plays are not too apt to be given television time because of the costs of rehearsal time and space and the value of air time, it must be said that less complicated programs have an excellent chance of making television, again primarily because of the almost universal appeal of young faces and voices engaged in something serious. If you have a lively subject like the 12-year-old who uncovers the remains of a local Indian settlement, or the group which discovers rare historical treasure in some unsuspected attic, or the girls who have learned how to hand-dip candles and are going to sell them for the holidays to the public to raise funds for the school's collections of community history materials, don't fail to let the program manager of the local TV station know. If he doesn't like the idea, he will tell you so, but the chances are that he has a ready-made spot three weeks from Monday.

The commercial UHF (ultra-high frequency) station today is more receptive to such programs than is the VHF (very high frequency) station. The educational TV station is apt to be most receptive of all, if you demand no elaborate stage props and need no rehearsal time, both of which are costly for a station that usually operates on a very tight budget. And educational TV is seemingly on the eve of a major expansion with federal aid. It is also always possible that a local industry or a bank will, for institutional advertising and community goodwill, sponsor such a program—buy the air time for your group if you really have something good.

The possibilities for adult-oriented programs are legion. They are subsidiary to the main goal of understanding how things happen (are made to happen) in the American society, economy, and polity, but they offer the students opportunities to share with the public both knowledge of the history of the community and knowledge of what is happening in at least part of the school curriculum—and in the process to achieve poise and stage presence and to share experiences that would otherwise not be available.

# 6

*Organization,
By-products, and
Caveats*

S HOULD the work in community materials be completely integrated into the social science—and art, music, theater, industrial arts, home economics, and physical education—curriculum, or should it be organized as an extracurricular club?

There are definite advantages to both alternatives. And since the alternatives are not mutually exclusive, maximum benefits can accrue from the simultaneous use of both approaches. The best solution for a given school or community has to be worked out in each instance on the scene by those involved in capitalizing on this rich and unique educational opportunity.

Integration will imply the primary use of community resources (1) to illustrate the generalizations of American history with local examples which, as has been noted, frequently depart from the national norm; (2) to increase understanding of American economy, society, and politics by studying intimate, immediate examples of how and why and who makes things happen in these fields of human endeavor. Local materials will be utilized as they illustrate points in the curriculum, whether the emphasis at a particular moment is on historical, or geographical, or governmental, or economic developments, whether the course is organized chronologically or topically or by "problems." Field trips will be restricted to those illustrating the workings of a business, a bank, the town government, etc.—the trips that illuminate points in the curriculum.

If the second alternative, the history or community club, is adopted, it will facilitate a more concentrated study of the community, taking a whole period of time or an entire topic to study over the year. This certainly will make possible the achievement of the interrelationships and insights which are so important: how a bit of local legislation may affect the business community; how the economics of the town affect its politics; how history may turn on a seeming accident of time and place; how history is made, how the order of events is affected, by people.

Collecting activities, to strengthen the library holdings in local materials and to add to the community resources for historical exhibits, can be carried on by either a class or a club, but really lie outside the formal curriculum. A History Fair can be held under either type of auspices, will probably work best under integration which gives an official status to the activity and so may facilitate the cooperation of other departments, but will probably produce the most interesting exhibits and projects if carried on as a club of students all of whom are interested in the work when they join the organization. The club, unless the class be primarily devoted to community history (a rarity above the elementary level), is the more apt to produce a booklet, or a marker program, or a pageant, or certain radio and adult programs. But all these can be produced by a class, too.

There is a tendency to use the separate club in rural schools, curricular integration in the city schools; but the exceptions are so numerous as to jeopardize the generalization. There really is no reason, despite all the demands on a teacher's time, not to use both: use the local illustrative material to give new life and meaning to American history; use the club for the continuing program of special projects in community history. The student in the classroom will gain new insights into the American experiment, new understanding of how this country has become what it is; the history-minded student in the club will have rare opportunities to achieve the further understandings which a more intimate and concentrated exposure to community history offers and to participate in the numerous related activities which will so greatly enrich his experience.

Several states have a statewide junior historians program, mostly organized by the state historical agency with the approval and support of the state education department.[1] If such a program exists in your state, investigate it carefully and see if it will not prove a useful adjunct to your own efforts in community history. Most of these programs have newsletters which pass on good ideas developed in one school to the other "chapters" in other schools. Useful books in the field are reviewed, as are new audio-visual materials. Most of these state programs publish magazines, consisting largely of articles written by junior historians. The existence of such a statewide outlet for students' historical papers is important: it encourages good writing, as it is a high and appreciated honor to get your essay into print in competition with the best that other students are doing all over the state. Several societies are publishing pamphlets and other material and making available slides, film strips, and circulating exhibit materials to participants in such programs. Participation, then, can be helpful. Participation also gives the students the sense of belonging to something bigger than the school or community, a fellowship of like-minded pupils all over the state all working on some aspect of the history of their own community.

---

[1] In addition, many local and county societies and museums across the country have programs for children which include regular meetings, awards, use of children as aides, special tours, and programs that enable youngsters to participate in activities typical of an earlier day.

These junior chapters have done some extraordinary things. They start in the elementary grades with the simple: something in the family, in the school, in the community. Inevitably, at least under an imaginative teacher, the simple object or item ties to something else. The next year they are ready for something a little more complex. By late high school they have the insight and perspective that can produce really substantial work. They have at this level written books which have been published. They have marked historic sites and set up historic tours in their communities. They have, all by themselves, preserved historic sites. They have even in at least one instance built a local museum. They have made significant archeological finds. And they have shared not only rich experiences but the unique insights localized history can give.

Some of these junior chapters have been extracurricular clubs; some of them meet regularly during social studies class hours. If this program exists in your state, join it.

But however the activity is organized, whether integrated or extracurricular, whether inside or outside of the junior historian movement, the vital point of the program is for the student to do it himself, not to listen to it from the lips of the teacher or even to read it from the largely nonexistent printed versions of local history. He can (must) do original work in community history to a degree not possible in any other field. In no other subject are the materials right at hand; in no other subject do they lead so close to understanding.

If in American history you want to know how Prohibition was accepted locally and what its impact was, there are plenty of people alive who lived through those troubled years. Go ask them, find out. If you are interested in the evolution of civil rights as it affects minority groups in this country, go ask people who have the information—the lawyer, the judge, the police official, the welfare worker. If you are interested in what the locality did in the Civil War, send the students to the 1860–65 file of local newspapers; look at the published lists of the Adjutant-General's office and pick out the local names; check the Civil War monument for the list of those who never returned; find out how all those Confederate veterans got buried in the local Northern cemetery, or Union veterans in that local Southern cemetery. Don't just listen. Don't just read. Go, find out. This is one of the very special merits of community materials: the freedom to explore for yourself, the lack of forced reliance on textbooks, the early venture into the delights and frustrations of research, gives this approach to the social studies unique value. It represents a different sort of learning experience. And it is a most important experience to supplement the formalized instruction which necessarily characterizes so much of the curriculum.

Basically, as indicated, such a program draws on the social sciences, especially history, geography, and civics (or government). But it can also draw on dramatics, on music, art, industrial arts, home economics, and can thus become an important thread tying together the work of various departments. This sort of reinforcement in learning is of very great value, yet it is seldom achieved. Our students go to one class for one subject. They go to another and find themselves in a totally different milieu. They go to a third and it is still different. They study English literature and modern American government and how to build a bench, one after another. Then they go to "gym." They could be studying American literature, American history, community studies, building display cases for the school museum, and learning the householding difficulties of the pioneer wife, and each subject would build on the others.

But the students are not the only ones to benefit from a program of community studies. A fascinating by-product is the involvement of the parents and other adults in the community. For better or worse, the student often will precede or supplement his library work with his parents' help. And parents, unhappy not to know something their children expect them to know, find themselves doing some research on their own. The mother may spend a few hours at the library, the father—hoping to acquire some knowledge painlessly—is apt to talk about it with his friends, or the men in the barbershop, or at the club, or at the corner waiting for the bus. Either way, the adult finds himself in the middle of a research project in local history. And the deeper he gets, the more he enjoys it, gets intrigued by it, and begins to reap the benefits of the understanding, perspective, and wisdom the historical approach has to offer. He becomes a better citizen because he knows at least something about the community and its history, and having learned that much he is apt to go on to further topics. At least he knows how to find out about them when he wants to. This, too, is all to the good.

Parents also get involved through field trips. The student enjoys a historic site or reconstruction, a restoration or museum, and wants to go again. Or he wants to visit the waterfront and watch that remarkable loading equipment again. Or he finds that he has forgotten whether the lumps of coal are first washed or sorted for size, and he wants to go back to the colliery and see. And so, at least until the students reach driving age, the parent or parents bundle the student and probably a couple of friends or brothers and sisters into the car and off they go—to find out, or to see the site or restoration, or to visit the museum.

Parents become involved through other special programs: through the History Fair, or the Folk Fair, through photograph identification nights, heirloom shows, or radio or television programs. They see, they approve, they become interested. It may be analogous to the involvement that comes with PTA membership, but this is on an intellectual level. It is an involvement that conceivably may be more interesting for both the parent and the teacher than some of the other existing avenues of mutual involvement. And most certainly it strengthens the learning process and experience for the students if the parents are personally interested in the subject matter and the activities.

One warning. Cooperate, don't compete, with the local historical society, the local museum, the local public library. Each has its own legitimate function, and if the three and the school are all active, a good deal of competition and quite a little friction are possible. Cooperate on the community inventory; cooperate on collecting; cooperate on putting library and museum articles alike where they will be of the most use to the most people and will have the best protection, especially if they are rare: cooperate on programming. Do programs for them on request; get their help and advice on your projects. The historical society might well supply specially informed guides (and perhaps additional cars and drivers) for a tour of historic sites in the area. You may even find interesting summer student jobs available with the society—as a guide in the society's historic house, as a pick and broom man at its summer archeological excavation, as clerical help in the office with mailings or filing or getting out the newsletter. There are large areas of mutual interest among school, library, historical society, and museum in this whole field of community study. Utilize this mutual interest, cooperate with each other, and each will go further together than alone. There is no pat formula for such cooperation. Circumstances vary in every locality. In some all four institutions will be strong and aggressive. In others one or more will be weak indeed or even nonexistent. The terms and form of cooperation have to be worked out in every community according to local circumstances and conditions. But cooperation is most desirable and should be carefully sought by all parties.

# EPILOGUE: HORIZONS UNLIMITED

THE preceding chapters have suggested the unlimited resources available in nearly every community for studying short range—under the microscope, if you will—the American experiment. How politics are conducted in and out of parties, how government operates in departments or councils or courts, how reforms are effected or lost. How business and commerce and communication are carried on, how capital is created, where money "comes from." Throughout there has been the sense of change, of development, from first settlement on: the changes in farming (or ranching or dairying), the changes in the processing and movement of goods, the changes in retailing, the changes in education and recreation. Change is the story of man's development; change is the story of a school or a company or a town; change is the essence of history. And the lesson that change is always with us is a valuable one for the student to master as early as possible.

Change is the work of individuals. We have seen how the study of community history emphasizes the continuing importance of the individual. This, too, is an important lesson to absorb early in life. The lack of an attractive foreseeable future, the sense of helplessness and hopelessness which seemingly afflicts so many of our teen-agers today, assumes its true perspective when confronted with the facts of what has happened and what is happening, who made it happen and who is making it happen in the average community today. Even in communities which are in economic or social decline, the fact that individuals and groups of people can change the course of community history is reassuring, might even stimulate a local teen-age Operation Bootstrap.

This focus on the continuing importance of the individual is also important in offering factual basis for mental resistance to the constant threat of further encroachments on the freedom of the individual, that paternalism in government which reaches its nadir in the so-called dictatorship of the proletariat and the police state.

81

It is important too as the young mind grapples with the implications of the Space Age. With over two hundred satellites in orbit as this is written, with plans under way for trips to other planets and ultimately into outer space, it is important to realize that for all the stargazing, man's future most likely remains tied to this planet, that man's work is done by men—by individuals in cities and hamlets, in communities like the one in which you live.

Further it is important in our highly mobile culture that the individual not become rootless. The adult newly come to a community is often the most eager to know its history, to understand the background of its present condition, to get roots down in the new home town. The new student is just as eager. The study of community history, the use of local materials, helps him sink roots into the local soil in a hurry. The psychological importance to the young mind of such understanding and such a sense of belonging despite recent arrival is by no means trivial.

Remember, too, that community history will often illustrate and bring alive the national movement or trend but will as often show local deviation from or even reversal of the national trend. The suspicion of the glib generalization thus created is another worthwhile bit of equipment for the student to acquire.

So all the values of history, queen of the social sciences, and of historical method—early experience with research techniques, and writing and publishing; field trips to reinforce classroom learning and outside research; the satisfaction of building study resources for one's colleagues and one's successors; the experience of sharing hard-earned knowledge both with one's peers and with adult groups directly or via radio or television; all these learning situations, all these values, all these experiences lie at hand for the student whose teacher has the initiative and imagination to use the rich mine of teaching tools and experiences which lie at his or her fingertips in the community.

Community resources put life into history. Localized history puts history into the life of the pupil. The materials are legion and of infinite variety; the possibilities are numberless; the horizons unlimited. And so to work.